DAN FLAVIN · ICONS

CORINNA THIEROLF and JOHANNES VOGT

Thames & Hudson

The authors wish to thank
Tiffany Bell and Stephen Flavin
for their invaluable and sustained support
of this publication.

C. T. and J. V.

Dan Flavin: ICONS

"But beyond structure and phenomena,
I have tried to infect my icon with
a blank magic which is my art."[1]

Dan Flavin, 1963

Between 1961 and 1964 Dan Flavin completed a group of eight works that he entitled *icons*. They form the seedbed of his method of working with "naked" fluorescent tubes and they mark a crucial conceptual turning point in his artistic development: Here, for the first time, he uses illuminants in the form of light bulbs, flashing lights and fluorescent tubes. Up until this point he expressed himself through drawing and painting, but after 1963 fluorescent tubes, which he joined together to make smaller objects or impressive installations, formed the predominant means with which he created art. That is why Flavin's *icons* are also an important link, they comprise works on the threshold between his paintings and his later light installations. They are the result of a search for artistic forms of expression beyond classical painting, they arise from the desire to "leave the picture behind."[2]

The modern preoccupation with the topic of icons has a long-standing history in 20th-century art. In 1915, Malevich declared his "black square" an "icon of my time"[3] and placed it in the famous "0.10 – Last Futurist Exhibition" in an upper corner of the room (fig. 1), in the exact place where icons can be found in orthodox households. Here are the roots of a conscious dialogue between the religious and the profane message in the picture. It feeds on the fertile tension between the classical panel on the one hand and icons on the other, between Eastern and Western understanding of images.

Like his Russian avant-garde predecessor, during a phase of intensive searching and rebellion against the classical definition of pictures, Flavin likewise returned to the basic conditions perceived to be governing icon painting. This raises questions about the form in which the religious pictures of the Orthodox Church are important for his *icons* and to what extent he takes up the Russian tradition.[4]

The early 1960s represent a time of radical change with regard to developments in art in North America. The new use of forms by artists such as Dan Flavin, Donald Judd, Carl Andre and Sol LeWitt is based – despite a range of differences between the artists – on the conscious call to produce objective and non-illusionist works of art which are free from subjective gestures.[5] This impulse was directed decidedly against the self-perception of Abstract Expressionist artists and was accompanied by the strict rejection of the validity of symbols and transcendence in all works produced.

However, in particular Dan Flavin's works reveal a mysteri-

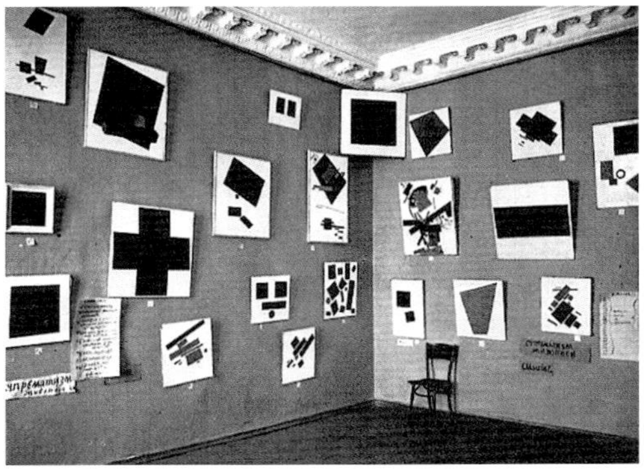

1 Installation shot of "0.10 – Last Futurist Exhibition", Petrograd 1915

ous ambiguity, and not only as regards the contrasting materiality of the real object (the brackets supporting the fluorescent tubes) and of the diffuse, fluorescing, dying light. It also refers to the permanent tension between the fact that the works are purely objects, as propagated by the artist (that is, their facticity beyond traditional symbol structures) and a partly concealed, partly visible approach, which opens up connotations over and beyond that which is purely factual.[6] Flavin's works lend themselves to direct perceptions of light, color and object and to the broad spectrum associated with traditional light imagery. Light therefore possesses – in addition to its philosophical implications in the ideas inherited from Plato – a spiritual dimension as the "lux perpetua", which is present in both Christian writings and in ecclesiastical liturgy. And in a figurative sense it stands for the intellectual desire for independence in Europe at the time of the Enlightenment (German: Aufklärung; French: des lumières), that is it stands for an act which demanded reason.

Given their pivotal position within Flavin's œuvre and the extensive material documenting their creation in the form of drawings and sketches, the *icons* as an early group of works offer a readily accessible opportunity to trace the genesis and nature of ambiguity in Flavin's works: the juxtaposition of light and object, of strict facticity and a message which transcends everything material.

Traditional icons

In a treatise from the 11th century by the Byzantine scholar Michael Psellos on an icon of the Crucifixion the following is written: "This inspired painting is indeed created from the artistic combination of such elements [of pure painting], but the appearance of life transcends this. And so, on the one hand, the icon lives to imitate (life) in art, and, on the other hand, it lives not just to reflect it, but to convey it in spirit under the influence of mercy (...) I wish therefore to conclude without a doubt that a higher power guided the hand of the icon painter and that this power was focused on the true prototype."[7] The effect of the icon is therefore far greater than simply being a pure reflection. The painter's hand was guided by a higher power, the picture is not a result of individual artistic genius. What causes icons to radiate in a way that is both clearly human, but at the same time divine? How can this be perceived by a modern viewer?

The Western understanding of images is part of a tradition which has developed since the early Renaissance. The Italian humanist Leon Battista Alberti characterized the Western panel picture as an "open window" to reality, a characterization which lasted well into modern times. The design of the picture with its central vanishing point is intended to suggest to the viewer that he is not looking at a two-dimensional surface, but, as it were, at a natural scene beyond the picture frame, exactly like looking out of a window. Producing a naturalist representation is therefore the most important commandment governing the "functioning" of Western images in the classical tradition.

By contrast, icons originate from an older, fundamentally different understanding of images. Committed to displaying only sacred themes in the iconography, they do not provide a representation of the holy figure they depict; they are not merely an image or a symbol of the figure, rather they show the *real presence* of the holy figure by means of the image. The saint is actually present qua the image. The icon thus develops its own individual corporality and at the same time constitutes a higher, divine reality.[8] Accordingly, the icon painter is not an artist as we understand the term in the West. He has a fixed set of rules to follow and he creates images not by drawing on his own aesthetic feeling, but by adhering to existing models. Since new icons are always based on their predecessors, this has resulted, on the one hand, in little development of their design. On the other hand, this guarantees that they correspond to the original image.

This belief is most intense when it concerns so-called *acheiropoieta*, i.e., things not made by hand. These are icons whose creation is possible without the presence of even an icon painter acting as a conduit – in a wondrous way the Divine has a direct effect on them.[9] The most famous example of this is the "Mandylion" or the "Vera Icon" which, according to legend, shows the face of Christ.[10] The details of this miracle vary depending on the Western and Eastern traditions. In the West, the legend of Saint Veronica is key; in the East it is connected to King Abgar of Edessa. Veronica wiped Christ's face with her veil and the features of the redeemer immediately appeared upon it. The artist commissioned by King Abgar to paint Christ's portrait was so dazzled by his face that he was unable to reproduce it. As a result of this, Christ imprinted his facial features onto the artist's clothes.[11] In both traditions, therefore, this representation is understood to be a true impression of the holy face and this is thus the archetype for relics touched by a saint. This marked the beginnings of a new type of representation, which shows only the head or the facial features of Christ.

The "Mandylion" shown here (fig. 2) originates from this tradition. The rectangular panel is coated with a gold ground which leaves only the face of Christ and the faint shape of the cross untouched. In the slightly indented, square surface of the image there is a precise circular form, which can be considered to be a halo. Both the form of the beard and hair and the facial features are consistent to the smallest detail with the traditional features of the Mandylion model. The overall impression is determined partly by the strict scheme of the compositional structure, which uses clear geometric formulae such as the circle, the square and the cross, but above all it is established by the radiance of the gold. By candlelight the observer would first perceive the magically sparkling gold ground and then the dark outlines of the face would open up within it. The *real presence* of Christ seems to shine directly out of the image through the gold. Real gold was used when making icons not only on account of its value, but also because its radiance – which seems to be of its own creation – reveals the direct presence of the saint. The divine appearance of Christ touches the observer directly through the rays of light, producing the feeling of a real and human presence.[12]

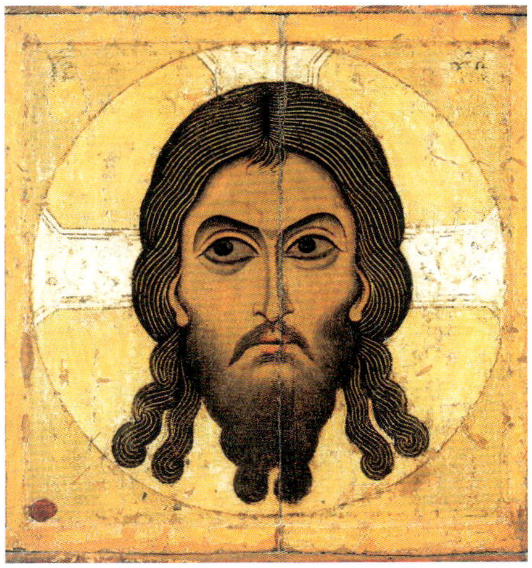

2 *Mandylion (Image of Edessa)*, Novgorod, 12th century, 30 5/16 x 27 7/8 in. (77 x 71 cm), Tretjakov Gallery, Moscow

Over and above the Byzantine tradition, the historical Mandylion is also the ur-icon of Christian images, as it testifies to the dual nature of Christ as man and as God. It is this theoretical artifice, namely so-called dyophysitism, that first meant images of the sacred could be made.[13] The Mandylion makes it clear that there was an icon at the beginning of all image production after the end of Classical Antiquity. At the latest with Alberti's theoretical treatises the understanding of the image differs fundamentally in the West as opposed to the East. Although the mimetic image tradition since the Renaissance is likewise inconceivable without the decisive theological turn of dyophysitism in the Early Middle Ages, with the ever stronger emphasis on "imitating nature" and the gradual growth in the notion of the artist as divine-like creator, a concept of producing images arose that severed its links with the tradition of the icon.

Flavin's *icons*

Dan Flavin's encounters with classical icons have been documented in a unique way. After studying the history of art at Columbia University from 1957 to 1959 he financed his life in New York by working as a museum attendant in the Museum of Modern Art (1959–60), then in the American Museum of Natural History and the Solomon R. Guggenheim Museum (1960–61). His interests were widespread, ranging from natural history to old masters and contempo-

3 *Christ in Glory*, icon, Russian (possibly Novgorod) painter, late 15th century, tempera on wood, 42⅛ x 30⅞ in. (107 x 78.4 cm), The Metropolitan Museum of Art, Gift of George R. Hann, 1944 (44.101)

rary art. Flavin wrote the following in a notebook concerning a visit to the Metropolitan Museum:

> "Last week in the Metropolitan, I saw a large icon from the school of Novgorod. I smiled when I recognized it. It had more than its painting. There was a physical feeling in the panel. Its recurving warp bore a history. This icon had that magical presiding presence which I have tried to realize in my own icons. But my icons differ from a Byzantine Christ held in majesty; they are dumb – anonymous and inglorious. They are as mute and undistinguished as the run of our architecture. My icons do not raise up the blessed Saviour in elaborate cathedrals. They are constructed concentrations celebrating barren rooms. They bring a limited light."[14]

Flavin dated the entry August 9, 1962, i.e., after he had designed and produced his first *icons*. As emphatically as he stresses the difference between this icon and his own work, as consciously as he distances himself from the area of friction between factuality and transcendence, it remains clear just how much he knows about the use and effective power of icons.

The icon that Flavin saw at the Metropolitan Museum in August 1962 was very probably "Christ in Glory" dating from the late 15th century (fig. 3) that can ostensibly be attributed to the Novgorod School.[15] The icon shows Christ on his throne surrounded by angels in a mandorla. His right hand is raised in a gesture of blessing, his left hand holds an open book with an inscription and his head is surrounded by a golden nimbus. In the four corners outside the mandorla are the four horsemen of the Apocalypse as representatives of the four evangelists of the New Testament. The icon corresponds to the classic "Majestas Domini" iconography intended to convey a portrait of the Redeemer in all his glory. The frontal view of Christ's face corresponds to the Mandylion type. Christ's upper body appears elongated and the schematic folds of his garments scarcely evoke an impression of plasticity. Nonetheless, the icon radiates that kind of equally magical and physical presence that Dan Flavin describes so accurately.

This sense of being face-to-face with a real person and not merely an illustration of one is also

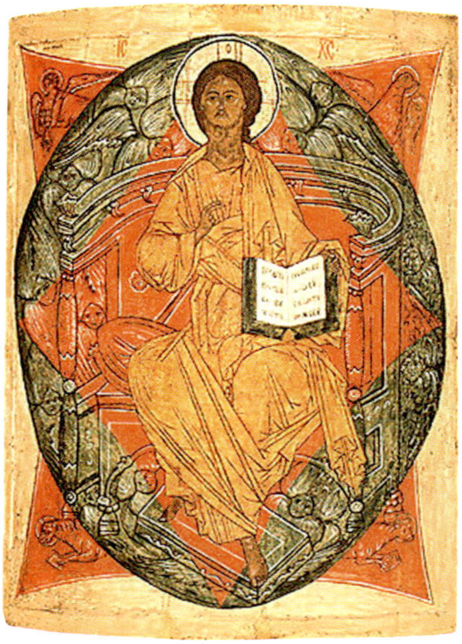

true of Flavin's *icons*. Whereas in photographs the pictorial quality of the wooden constructions measuring between 25 x 25 in. and 44 x 44 in. dominates, when confronted directly the works assume an almost physical presence, as they encroach upon the viewer's perceptual space, conveying, in their three-dimensionality, the impression of factual objectuality. The downward-directed light of the tubes extends the work's scope of effect to the surrounding room. Not only does the viewer stand opposite the work of art, he can, so to speak, enter it and thus become a part of it.

All the *icons* are made with great skill, with the craftsmanship particularly being evidenced on the reverse (see plates).[16] A robust structure held together by glue and screws and consisting of pine struts supports the front and the narrow sides of the rectangular boxes, which tend to be made of Masonite fiberboard and are painted with oil or acrylic on a Gesso ground.[17] While the first three *icons* have a depth of 5–6 in., the later *icons* are as much as 10–11 in. deep. Another overarching feature they all share is Flavin's painstaking documentation of the work. The labels on the backs not only state in careful handwriting the title and size of the particular work, but also list precisely the materials used, in part even stating the exact paint used, and in the case of the fluorescent tubes even adding "PURCHASED AT MACY'S DEP'T STORE".[18] All entries are made in upper-case letters, which almost suggests that Flavin wanted to pre-empt any mystification as regards his *icons*. His intention was clearly to enumerate each individual step in the production and all the materials used, fully in line with the creed he later formulated as "it is what it is and it ain't nothin' else."[19]

Flavin's conceptual considerations on the *icons* span the entire period from 1961 to 1963, in one case even into 1964 (*icon VII*). In a 5 x 3 in. ring-bound pad that he always took with him, he made countless sketches and drawings that focus not only on the eight pieces then realized but also on ones he never made.[20] As late as 1964 and 1965, in the period after the "gold diagonal" of May 25, 1963 (see p. 77), i.e., after his first piece not entailing an object, he designed new *icons*. Flavin focused on the idea as such for a long while to come. The group of the eight *icons* realized is thus only the tip of the iceberg, the body of the work as a whole is to be sought in the many-part structure of fleeting sketches and detailed studies. In a prolonged process, the first ideas condense and lead finally to the production of a work.[21]

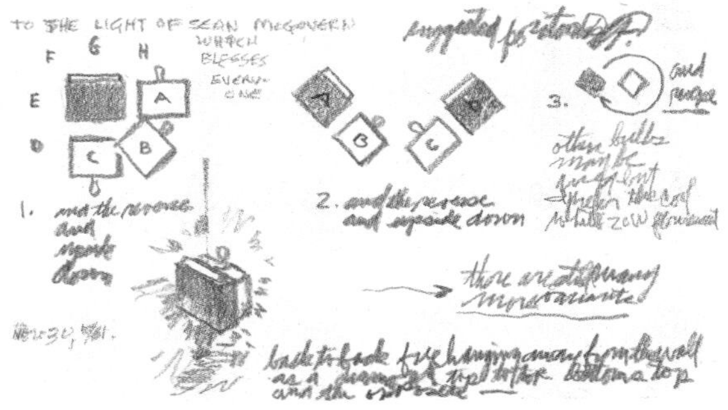

4 Sketchbook drawing, 11/30/1961

Although the eight pieces shared the same underlying concept, we cannot speak of a group of works in the sense of a coherent unit. Flavin did not define the number of pieces in advance. And the aspect of the serial group as came to bear in his later work is not to be sensed here, as the sequence of the eight *icons* does not entail mere modulations of one and the same principle derived in rational/conceptual terms from one another, as each piece stands on its own, developed from a specific context and the result of a long creative process.

5 Sketchbook drawing, 3/20/1962

icon I & *icon II*

In the sketchbooks of 1961 there are numerous drafts for *icon I (the heart) (to the light of Sean McGovern which blesses everyone)* and *icon II (the mystery) (to John Reeves)*. *Icon I* consists of a red painted 25 x 25 in. large square wooden construction whose dimensions are presumably derived from the horizontally positioned and shortest available fluorescent light tube. It gives off red light. *Icon II* is made to identical dimensions and is painted yellow. On the upper side, right of the center Flavin has attached a ceramic holder for a light bulb, which gives off yellow light in correspondence with the color of the object. Both works were completed in 1961, but *icon II* was painted again in 1962. They were conceived jointly over a longer period of time. In the first two *icons* he produced, Flavin investigates the various options for combining in the one instance a painted structure and fluorescent tube and in the other a painted structure and a light bulb.

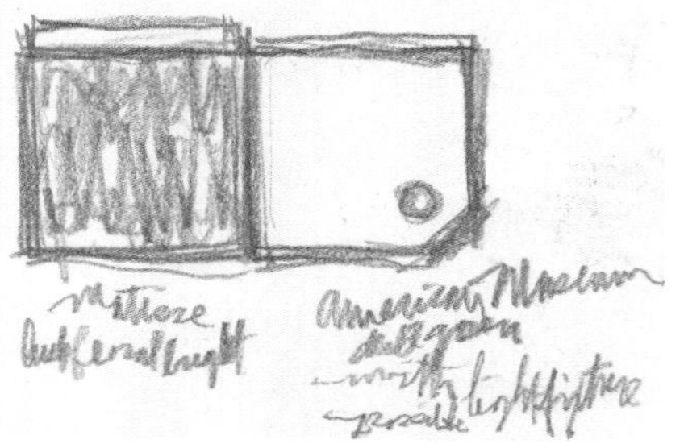

6 Sketchbook drawing, probably 1961

The works are very closely interrelated in Flavin's sketches. With one exception *icon I* is always positioned left of *icon II*. In a sketch dated November 30, 1961 (fig. 4) both works are shown in a variety of different presentation options. Flavin uses the expression "back to back" to describe the two *icons* standing on the floor with the rectangular objects joined back to back. Above this you see conceptions for wall-mounted works in which the works are tilted, or even a system of varying presentation forms of the two works presented in clockwise fashion. A sketch produced a few months later (fig. 5) entitled *icon I & II* already features the designs for *icons* executed later on (from top to bottom: *icon III, IV* & *VI* but also two that were not realized). While all the other works are depicted singly, Flavin presents his first two versions side by side (uppermost). The origin of this idea seems to lie in an even earlier sketch that can be associated with an entire series of jotted ideas that Flavin refers to with the epithet "American Museum". He must have made these sketches during his stint as museum attendant in the American Museum of Natural History; Flavin was employed here from May 1960 to October 1961. A particularly large number of sketches was produced between June and October 1961, when Flavin did not have his own studio.[22] Presumably the sketch on the customary ring binder paper (fig. 6) was produced during this period and consequently several months before the sketches discussed previously.[23] It shows *icon I* with dark hatching on the left side and next to it a second *icon*, which recalls the later *icon VI* on the right side. Evidently at this point in time it was not yet certain that *icon II* would be executed, yet the sketch produced in November of the same year already shows the realized version which according to Flavin was completed in 1961. A further reminder of his time in the American Museum is evident in the person to whom *icon I* is dedicated, namely Sean McGovern, an Irish emigrant, who worked in the American Museum at the same time as Dan Flavin. *Icon II* is dedicated to a friend of the artist, whom he met at Columbia University.[24]

Excursus: titles and dedications

With the exception of two titles (*icon V* & *VII*), all eight *icons* follow the same naming system: Firstly, they bear the descriptive title "icon", followed by the respective number, and they carry dedications to persons from Flavin's private life or to public figures. Secondly, there is an addition as in *icon I* and *II* "the heart" and "the mystery", respectively. We are familiar with this practice from earlier assemblage works or watercolors by the artist. However, it is singular for those works featuring fluorescent tubes.[25] Works created after the *icons* are always "untitled" and are almost always given a dedication. Epithets such as "the heart" and "the mystery" no longer crop up. What is more, Flavin writes these descriptions on the rear of *icon I* and *II* above the word "icon"; as such, this prominence lends them a significance that goes beyond arbitrary or chance circumstances of production, and is more than a simple distinction to other works.[26]

While in the first *icon* "heart" seems to be directly reflected in the use of red paint and the red fluorescent tube, in the second *icon* the connection between the yellow paint, yellow light bulb and "mystery" is not immediately apparent. The connection becomes possible once you realize that Dan Flavin described the light given off by yellow fluorescent tubes as "gold".[27] Consequently, you find in the yellow of the bulb and in the yellow color of the box an echo of the mysterious glow of the gold ground featured in classic icons as an indication of the divine.

icon III

The view of Flavin's *icons* in the Pinakothek der Moderne (see p. 72/73) shows the first three works in chronological order from left to right. The wooden construction of *icon III (blood) (the blood of a martyr)* is painted with dark-red paint and has the same dimensions as *icon I & II*. There is a bulb on the upper side, which is shifted right of center as in *icon II*, and a fluorescent light in standard red tone is fixed to the underside in the same manner as in *icon I*. The effect: it looks as if Flavin had placed his first two works over each other and fused them to a new work. Here he tries out the interplay of bulb and fluorescent tube on an object. A difference in the construction is the linoleum lining of the box on the right side and on the upper side from the left edge up to the bulb. As this lining is missing on the right of the bulb and on the left side, the color produced respectively on the right and left side also varies. On the left side what emerges is a dark violet layer, which is much darker than the color of the actual surface. Evidently, Flavin has engaged in experimentation here and has also worked the sides of the object. While the first two *icons* are closer to the conventional image – you could say that the frontal picture surface extends beyond the side edges – in this instance we find a construction and composition principle which treats every element of the box closed on five sides separately.

A photograph from Flavin's studio (fig. 7) attests to these experiments. What we see is a first version of *icon III* on the right side of the first two works. Once again Flavin has chosen a means of presentation that features the objects with sides touching. His third *icon* is painted in a darker hue that appears black and evidently the sides have not been lined with linoleum. The most striking difference to the later version is that there is a white fluorescent tube on the underside of the box while on the upper side there is a much smaller bulb than the standard bulb to be seen to the left.

The choice of title departs from Flavin's usual scheme. Strictly speaking there is no dedication, as no specific martyr is named and the dedicating "to" is omitted. Rather, the words "the blood of a martyr" are an addition to the general title "blood".[28] And indeed, the color of paint is reminiscent of spilt blood, which enters into a dialog with the more lively, lighter red tones of the colored light of the bulb and the fluorescent tube. However, it must be said that the title unfolds its connection to the realized work only in this later and final version. It can therefore be assumed that choice of title coincided with the red-colored painting over. Indeed, within the *icons* group this is the only work in which different colors are layered on top of each other in a creative process. Flavin himself refers to yellow, brown and violet.[29]

icon IV

icon IV (the pure land) (to David John Flavin [1933–1962]) differs strikingly in terms of materiality, style and appearance from the first three *icons*. The work shown here is a second version of *icon IV*, created

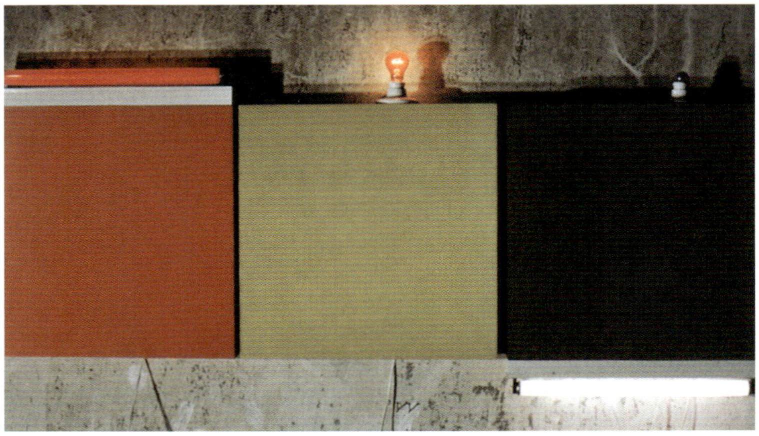

7 Left to right: *icon I, II & III*, 1962. Installation view in the artist's studio, around 1962

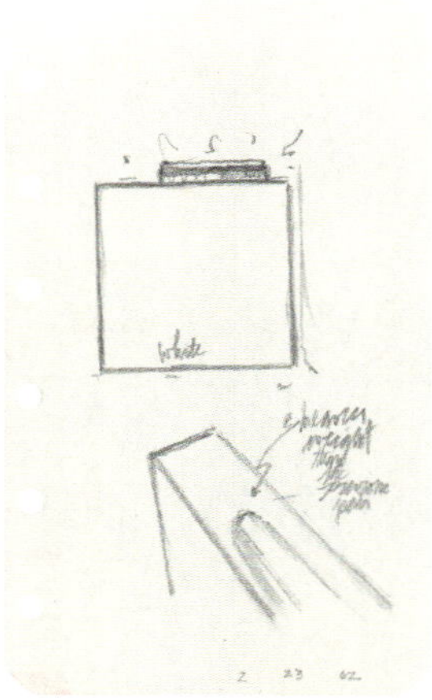

8 Sketchbook drawing, 2/23/1962

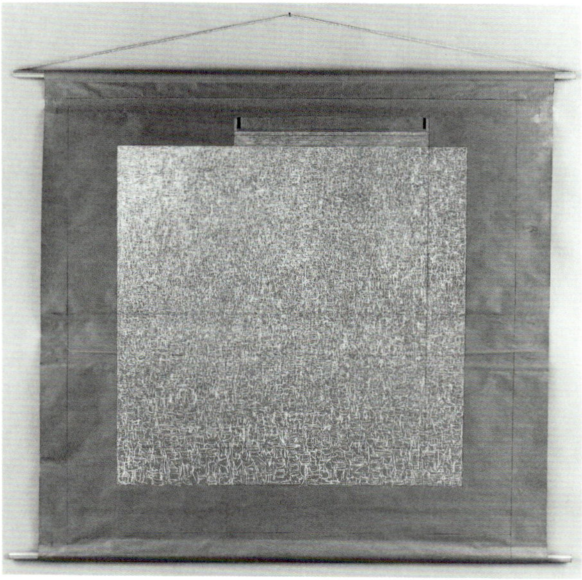

9 *full-scale diagram for icon IV*, 1962 (from June 14, 1962), white grease pencil and pencil on brown paper, $65\frac{1}{4} \times 65\frac{3}{8}$ in. (165.7 x 166 cm)

with Flavin's agreement for the 1969 retrospective in Ottawa. Given the distinct, dated sketch material, the original work can only have been completed after mid-July 1962. It was damaged in an exhibition on display in Green Gallery in New York in January 1963 and was subsequently destroyed.[30]

With its $44\frac{1}{2}$ in. long sides and a depth of around 11 in., *icon IV* is almost twice as big as the previous *icons*. Furthermore it is noticeable for a totally different surface structure. In this case Flavin did not use plain wood and paint it, but used white plastic material placed on wooden boards, which was available under the name "Formica". For the first time the surface has no texture, it is totally smooth, sterile. On the top there is a bright white fluorescent tube – once again the smallest standard unit –, that causes the white appearance to seem even whiter.[31] In its aseptic aesthetics *icon IV* differs from the seven other versions. It refuses most clearly the conclusion that there is a designing element in play and distances itself furthest from the classic idea of a work of art.[32]

The presumably first study is dated February 23, 1962 (fig. 8). It already bears the description "white" and has the fluorescent tube set slightly in from the edge of the picture on the right-hand side, as was actually the case in the version completed with plastic. Flavin changed his mind with regard to the positioning of the fluorescent tube. This is demonstrated by the dual portrayal of the work on a sketch pad on July 18, 1962 (fig. 10, at the bottom in the middle), in which the illuminant appears once flush with the upper right-hand edge and once to the left of the center. The positioning the artist ultimately decided on can already be seen in a diagram made in June 1962 featuring a true size illustration of *icon IV* (fig. 9): Two lines running parallel to the lower right edge of the picture indicate that Flavin extended the corpus of the *icon* there in each case by 5 inches. The square enlarged in this way caused the illuminant to be brought in – and the diagram that originally had curiously shifted to the left was now exactly in the middle of the sheet of paper. [33] Alongside the numerous sketches the true size graphic portrayal is an indication of the care Flavin put into creating his *icons*.

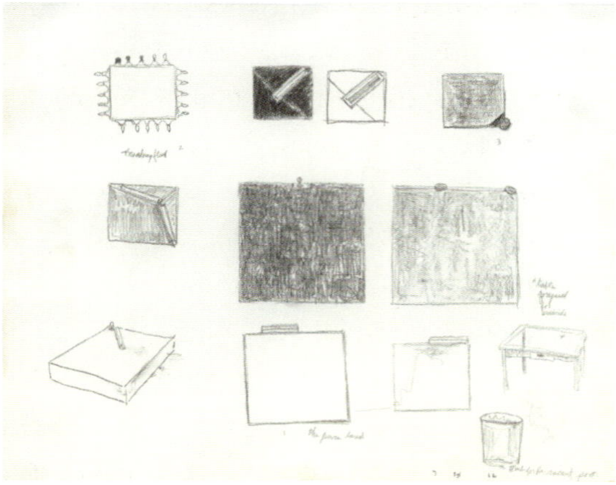

10 *untitled*, 1962, (7/18/1962), pencil on paper, $11 \times 13\frac{15}{16}$ in. (27.9 x 35.4 cm)

The artist himself provided the information that the *icon* he devoted to his twin brother, who died on October 8, 1962,[34] contained a reference to the use of white in Chinese funerals.[35] The term used in the title "the pure land" would also be appropriate in this context. It first appears in Flavin's work in the June 1962 diagram already mentioned (fig. 10). In Japanese Buddhism, the "pure land of the West" is the last station in a person's life before entering Nirvana. The link to oriental philosophy is reflected in

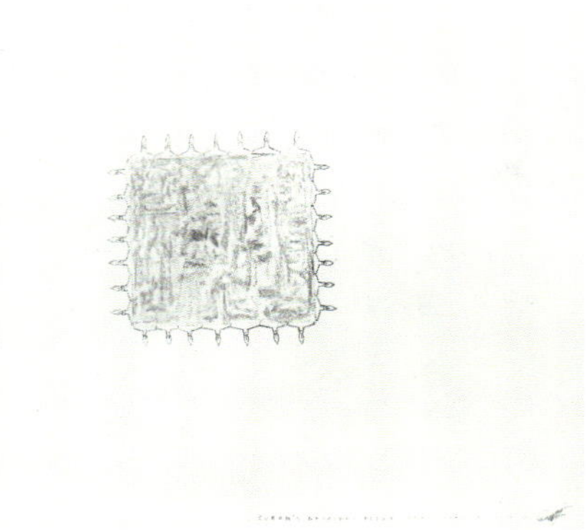

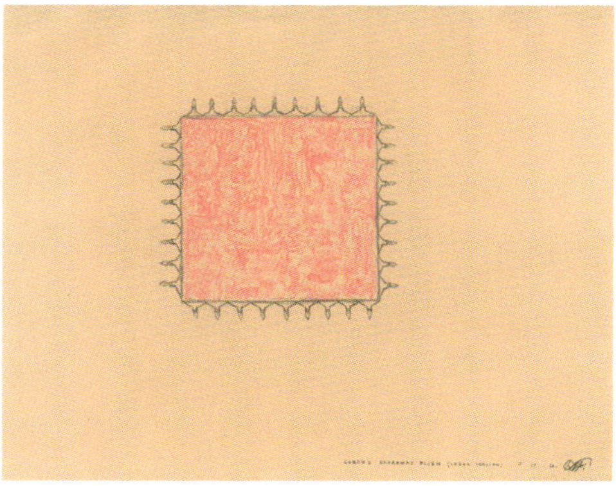

the style of the large-format diagram (fig. 9). Flavin designed this life-size study like an East Asia scroll picture with the calligraphy boasting a fine color structure.

The title indicates his knowledge of religious customs in the Far East, and he blends this source with references to the orthodox icon and the occidental image, thereby finding a formulation that extends beyond each and every archetype.

Furthermore, deliberations on the pure white radiance of this work appear to be mirrored in a polished study (fig. 13) for an *icon* that was never made. It is referred to as "the white and the black" and displays a black structure with a slanting surface positioned on the ground, onto which a white fluorescent tube is attached diagonally to the sides of the square. Two weeks earlier this project had already appeared next to a white counterpart in a diagram (fig. 10, at the top in the middle). Flavin's allusion to the Chinese color of mourning is reflected here in the dichotomy of Eastern and Western culture, almost as if he wanted to confront them with each other. Flavin did not put the concept of a pair of *icons* in white and black into practice. However, the relationship between the compositional idea and the later *icon VII* is striking.

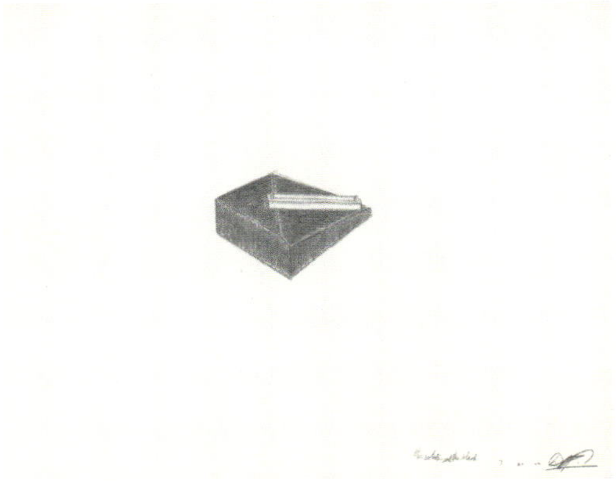

icon V

With its 32 in. sides *icon V (Coran's Broadway Flesh)* is the second largest object in the *icons* work group. It is painted pink and on all four sides features seven candle-shaped light bulbs in the familiar porcelain holders. In this œuvre the title and the dedication merge, as "Coran" is a person Flavin knew personally. In a February 1963 letter the artist himself wrote about the work as follows:

> "I would like to inform your interest about this work which I regard as summary for more than a year's research. Coran's Broadway Flesh is my fifth electric light icon. It is an emblem…it stands for a young English homosexual who loved New York City. What I have made for him is a square block loaded with flesh tint, mechanized by lamps, and bounded by excurrent tips of clear glass glister. But beyond structure and phenomena, I have tried to infect my icon with a blank magic which is my art. I know that this is hard to cope with, but, if I have succeeded,

11 *final study for Coran's Broadway Flesh* (small version), 1962, pastel and pencil on paper, 11 x 13⅞ in. (27.9 x 35.2 cm)

12 *study for Coran's Broadway Flesh* (large version), 1962, pastel and pencil on paper, 11 x 13⅞ in. (27.9 x 35.2 cm)

13 *untitled (the white and the black)*, 1962 (from 7/20/62), pencil on paper, 11 x 13 15/16 in. (27.9 x 35.4 cm)

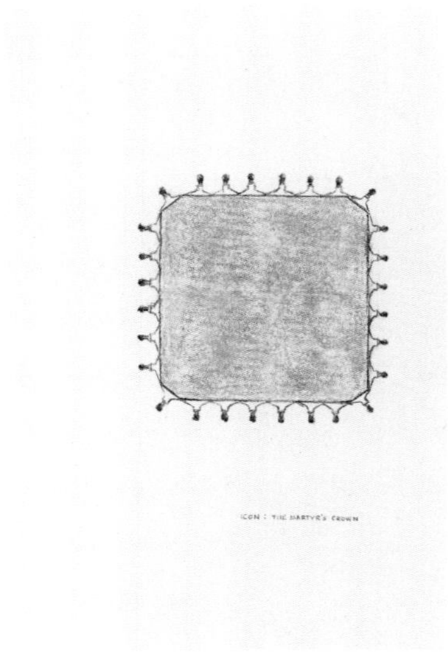

14 *untitled (icon: the martyr's crown)*, 1963, pastel and pencil on paper, 11 x 6⅞ in. (27.9 x 17.5 cm)

Coran's Broadway Flesh will hold you simply, succinctly."[36]

Flavin gave the square box a flesh tint and immediately shattered this anthropomorphic allusion through a garland of glittering light threads behind glass sheaths. It is evident from Flavin's words just how convinced he was of the power of impact of his works. At the same time it is evident that alongside the stringency and rationality of the composition there is also room for contextual dimensions, for symbolic power.

In the upper left-hand corner the diagram dated July 18, 1962 (fig. 10) reveals a study for the fifth *icon* that is already labeled "Broadway flesh". It is obvious that Flavin played with the idea of attaching various holders with the relevant types of bulb on the top side of the work, whereas on each of the other three sides there are five candle-shaped bulbs visible. So at the time this was still a "work in progress". Some two months later Flavin made two diagrams with the same date that already display *icon V* as it was in fact later produced. The first (fig. 11) shows the work with seven bulbs per side – as it indeed later featured –, the second, on the other hand, with nine bulbs on each side (fig. 12). Once again the artist is testing the work's appearance and proportions, taking into account the relationship between the corpus, side lengths, and number of bulbs using the medium of drawing.

In a study for an *icon* that was never completed (fig. 14) the symbolic valence and figurative language of these early works is expressed particularly significantly. Flavin gave it the subtitle "the martyr's crown".[37] The study is dated January 31, 1963 and as such was produced shortly after *icon V* was finished. Here, Flavin references the pattern of the surrounding light bulbs in *icon V*, but slants the four corners' construction such that a more circular structure emerges. Whereas *icon II* seems to allude to the effect of the gold base of classic icons, this is a clear formal and symbolic reference to the crown of thorns. Flavin himself said that he began work on the œuvre but then discarded it.[38]

icon VI

icon VI (Ireland dying) (to Louis Sullivan) references in the length of the sides the first three *icons* again, though at 10 in. in depth the sculptural impact experimented with in *icons IV & V* is retained. The box is painted green on all sides. The bottom left-hand corner of the front is slanted with a sharp 45 degree edge.[39] On the slant a red flashing light beneath a dark green glass cover and aligned to the ground is attached. Here, Flavin is playing with the complementary contrast between the two colors used; almost humorously he emphasizes that with this work he is breaking down the stringency of his square framework. By eliminating one corner he also creates awareness of the perfection of the square boxes.

On the above-mentioned experimental page with a drawing (fig. 10) we find an advanced study of *icon VI* in the upper right-hand corner, which envisaged an even bigger light bulb for the work. In late 1962 the deliberations became conclusive studies, though the *icon* itself was not made until early 1963. On a drawing dated November 28 (fig. 15) the title "Ireland dying" appears for the first time. Two weeks later a final drawing (fig. 16) emerges that has

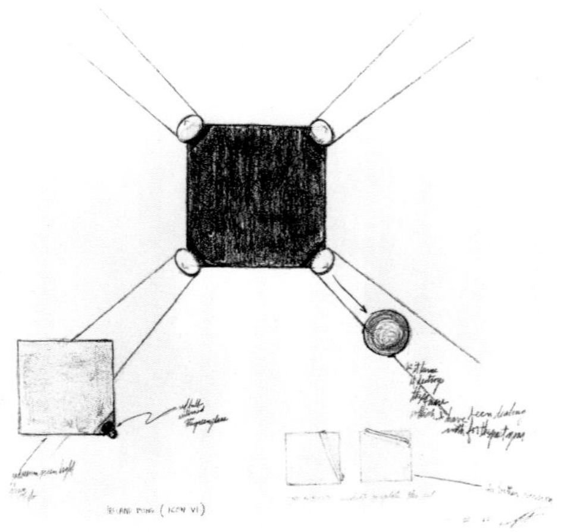

15 *untitled (studies for icons VI, VII, and VIII)*, 1962, pencil on paper, 11 x 13⅞ in. (27.9 x 35.2 cm)

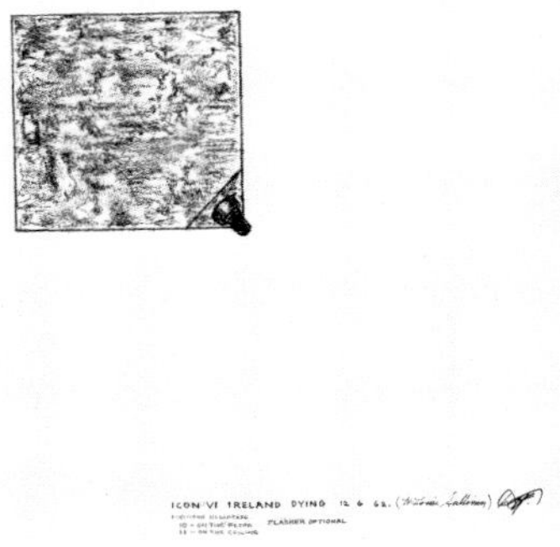

16 *icon VI (Ireland dying)*, 1962, pastel and pencil on paper, 11 x 14 in. (27.9 x 35.6 cm)

icon VI in the middle of the picture and now bears the dedication to the American architect Louis Sullivan (1856–1924). The title contains a reference to Flavin's family's Irish roots. Since 1949 the "emerald isle" had been experiencing constant political unrest and the division of the country had left a deep wound. In retrospect the term "dying Ireland" would appear to be an all too accurate vision of the bloody Troubles that occurred in the 1970s with the IRA playing a bigger role. With its endless never changing flashing rhythm the flickering little red light behind the green glass in Flavin's work symbolizes the hopelessness of the Irish plight.

icon VII

In *icon VII (via crucis)* the rectangular box structure, whose dimensions correspond to those of *icon VI*, is broken up in the upper right-hand corner by a slant, which on the photograph is particularly emphasized by the asymmetrical edge running from top left to the middle of the right-hand side. Along this edge the slanting surface of the wooden construction is fitted with a white fluorescent tube attached so that the tube holder is aligned perfectly with the edge. It emits white light that stands out in maximum contrast to the black background.

In the bottom half, the drawing dated November 28 (fig. 15) already reveals two small studies for the seventh *icon*. Here, Flavin places two alternative drafts next to each other: in the one on the left the tube is aligned more vertically, in that on the right more horizontally. Despite the more pointed angle at which it is affixed, the second version corresponds pretty much exactly with the work that was completed later. Flavin would seem to have already opted for this version, as beside it he noted: "the better version". In this quick, tiny record one can see how for Flavin the square, cubic shape is the decisive basic structure of his *icons*. Starting from this basic structure he plays through the conceptual idea of fluorescent tubes placed over a slant being an addition to this square shape in two alternative constellations so as to be able to make a definite decision on one of them. In terms of shape however, the artist allows himself hardly any leeway at all.

Another diagram dated January 24, 1963 (fig. 17) shows the seventh *icon* in the middle at the bottom of the picture and bears the title "via crucis" (Latin for "Stations of the Cross"). In this highly detailed version the hatching already indicates the dark coloring of the work. This is not an experimental sketch, as the design and title have already been decided. Yet here too one can observe how the slanting edge meets up directly with the upper left-hand corner, thereby differing from the completed version. Here the final work reveals a more exciting situation: Breaking out of the strict geometry, the edge's top cut surface has shifted further to the right, such that the corner of the box is preserved. This is quite clearly an artistic decision that Flavin only decided on during the creative process.

At the same time the design marks yet another facet of Flavin's pictorial idiom. The title and composition of this work rely closely on each other. When the artist, by

17 *untitled (to be and would be icons)*, 1963, pencil on paper, 11 x 13¾ in. (27.9 x 35 cm)

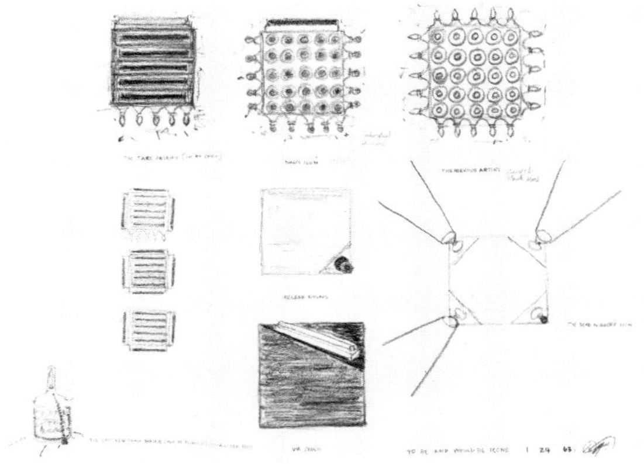

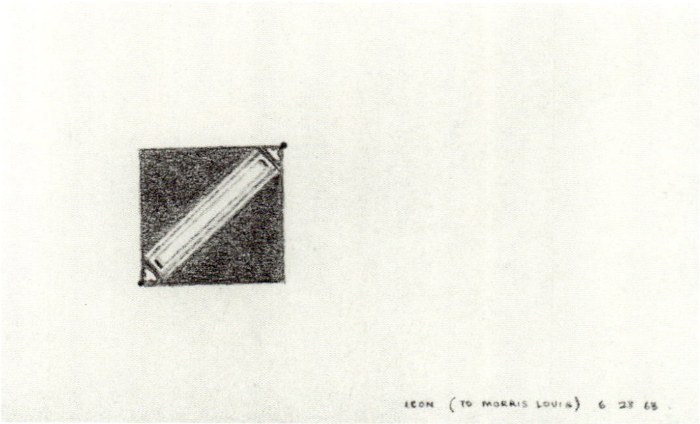

18 *for an icon (to Morris Louis)*, 1963, pencil on paper, 3 x 4 15/16 in. (7.6 x 12.5 cm)

means of his recently discovered medium, fluorescent tubes, symbolizes walking along a route, this appears to be visual onomatopoeia. The heading, left in Latin, references the Passion of Christ, the plight the Redeemer had to endure ascending Golgotha, the crucifixion hill, bearing the cross on his shoulders. Flavin translates his associations with the Stations of the Cross into highly abstract language, but provides just enough methods of interpretation that perception of the object by the title leads to a set of thoughts that extends beyond the purely factual materiality of the work.

Another study for an *icon* that never actually materialized likewise reveals a clear relationship between pictorial language and title. A drawing dated June 28, 1963 (fig. 20), in other words a whole month before the "Diagonal of Personal Ecstasy" was completed, shows an advanced individual study for a work Flavin entitled "icon (to Morris Louis)". The dedication is to the American artist who died in 1962, whom artists such as Judd and Flavin held in high esteem, particularly on account of his treatment of the diagonal.[40] The study reveals a dark square base, whose corners are diagonally connected from bottom left to top right diagonal by a fluorescent tube, at the ends of which there is a light bulb attached.[41] The visual reference to Morris' last paintings, particularly to "No End" (fig. 19) is striking.

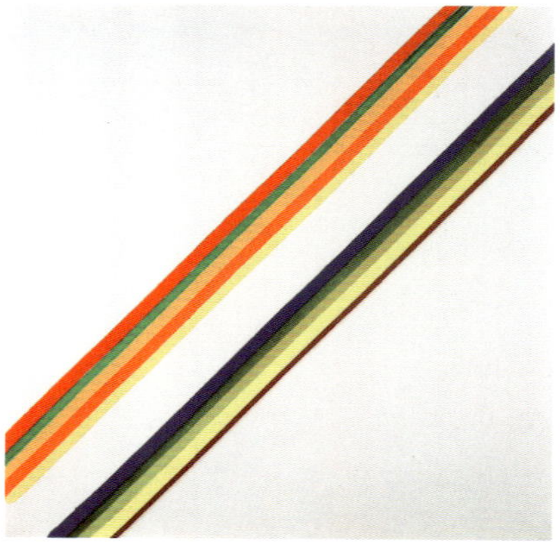

19 Morris Louis, *No End*, 1962, acrylic resin (Magna) on canvas, 63 x 63 in. (160 x 160 cm), Estate of the artist

The scope of reference Flavin establishes with his *icons* is by no means geared solely to religious sources. Far more his method of working is characterized by the fact that he can transport both profane and spiritual contents using the same means.[42]

icon VIII

The eighth and final œuvre in the work group under consideration bears the title *icon VIII (the dead nigger's icon) (to Blind Lemon Jefferson)* and in terms of dimensions follows on directly from *icons VI & VII*, analogous to the comparable dimensions of the first three *icons*, as is quite clearly visible in a view of an installation in the 1964 exhibition in Kaymar Gallery (fig. 20). Here the artist slanted all four corners of the square box in the same way and in each case put a flashing light on the slanting surface. The corpus of the *icon* is painted yellow and, when viewed from the front, creates the impression of a square having been entangled with a rhombus. It is this interplay between the horizontal/vertical pattern, which all *icons* feature, and its penetration by the diagonal on all four corners that in its formal appearance makes Flavin's last *icon* the most agitated, but also diverse work.[43] The irregular flashing of the red lights plays a considerable role in this. Though, when observed individually, each does flash in a regular rhythm, when viewed together, a chaotic confusion emerges. What is perceived is an uncontrolled flickering of the lights, as the breaks in between each

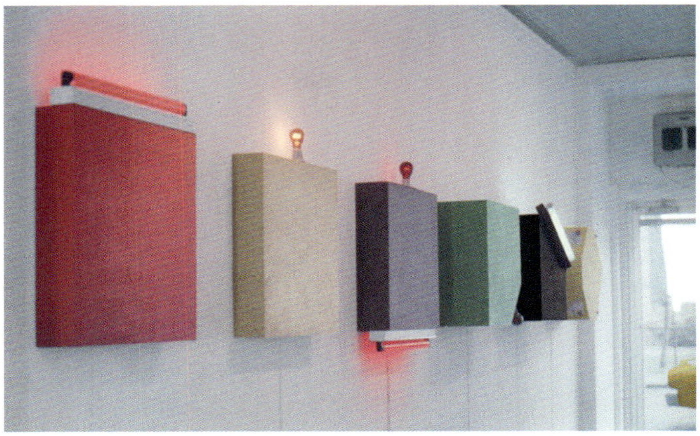

20 Left to right: *icon I, II, III, VI, VII & VIII*. Installation view at Kaymar Gallery, New York, 1964 (a total of seven icons was on display)

bulb lighting up are too short for the observer to immediately recognize the order in the chaos.

The title and dedication blend in this work. Flavin refers to the famous blind Blues musician Lemon Jefferson (1893–1929). While working on this *icon* the artist listened to one of his albums.[44] Once again the relationship between the work's picture and title are striking. On the one hand the musician's first name, Lemon, is mirrored in the color. On the other, on account of the work one is put in an almost musical mood. The lights flashing at alternating intervals resemble punctuated notes; the overall appearance even becomes syncopated rhythms. In this final work – in the previous ones it was already in evidence – an important element in Flavin's later creative method came into effect: He demands of observers that they perceive his works over time. From a single glance the work might well be able to be grasped in terms of its formal appearance but not, however, in its complexity and as such not as a whole.[45] Just as in the case of the installations, observers are called on to walk around the rooms, so the eighth *icon* only develops into a whole through a lengthy perception process. Just as musical sounds become comprehensible only through intervals in time, and a tone only gains meaning through the interplay with the next and the next but one, here too the work must be accessed in the course of the observation process. When photographing this *icon,* the lens was left open just long enough for all the lights, even the one in the top left-hand corner, to be lit up once and as such appear to be constantly illuminated – a sight that in this form the work itself can never provide. The lights operate independently; each of the individual signals claims its own space, a time that is reserved for it, to then begin interplay with the other flashing lights.

The *icons* in reflection on Flavin's early work

Outstanding parallels between the individual *icons* become apparent if we view the eight works as a whole. Even though at a first glance these works seem to lack reference, are abstract and often viewed in perspective of later works, they spawn an almost naïve directness as regards title and image: the red heart; the golden, yellow secret the *icons* keep; the martyrs' scarlet red blood; the white, mourning *icon*; the flesh-colored incarnate *icon*, clad in Broadway-glitter; the green, dying Ireland; the diagonal "Via Crucis" and the musical *blues icon* in yellow and red. They constitute a complex denseness of rich references to the contents. Through these abstract works, clear links can be made to the source of inspiration as well as the character of the (intended) message of the *icons*. Yet they are not so abstract that we cannot construe connections, albeit as the product of an active effort. The artist's works that were developed only a short time before the *icons* – such as assemblages of found materials or watercolor paintings of poems – are far clearer in terms of references. Evidently,

Flavin's main intention was to reach a new level of abstraction with these *icons*. But where exactly can one place these *icons*, and what makes these objects icons? How can the titles be read from within the works?

The piece "Juan Gris in Paris (adieu Picabia)" (fig. 21) was created between 1960 and 1962 and gives a clue here. The rectangular fiberboard is covered with blue oil paint irregularly in a sculptural and relief-like way. In the center left of the picture a crushed can is positioned, connected to the top margin of the picture by two red strips of paint. A horizontal red bar is located in the lower part of the picture. Now it is of interest that Flavin, having already begun this work in 1960, framed it later in 1961 and 1962 with sidewalls 3 in. in depth.[46] Thus, at a point in time after the first *icons* had been completed he reworked this older piece and gave it a box-like structure that is reminiscent of the *icons'* underlying principle. Yet the artist did not connect this piece to the group of *icons* – this too, immediately becomes apparent to the viewer. Where exactly is the distinction?

First of all, the sidewalls of "Juan Gris in Paris (adieu Picabia)" are smaller in width than the earlier *icons* completed in 1961. Its status as an object is not yet as clearly emphasized as with the *icons*. The gestural design of the surface stands in contrast to the schematic form of painting used for the *icons* and appears more painterly.[47] Also, a crushed can is attached to the Juan Gris piece and the piece reveals a well-considered composition of red stripes over the blue ground. Here, deliberate artistic decisions were required that through visual choices led to aesthetic positions. Precisely this compositional procedure was something that Dan Flavin and Donald Judd declared they had overcome in an interview in 1964.[48]

21 *Juan Gris in Paris (adieu Picabia)*, 1960–62, crushed can and oil on masonite, and acrylic on balsa, 19⅞ x 3³⁄₁₆ in. (50.4 x 61 x 8.1 cm)

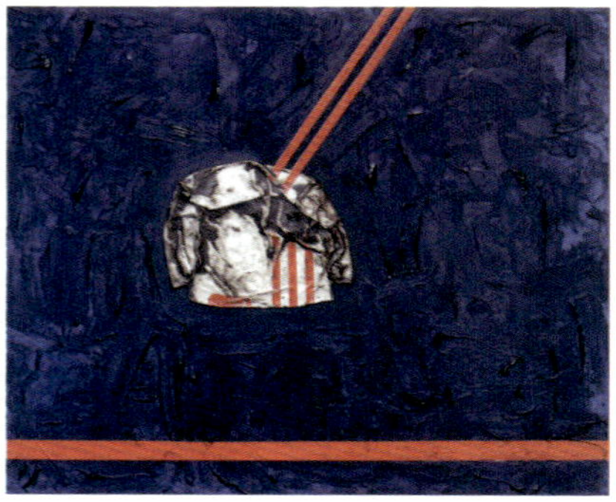

In this light and in contrast to the basic rectangular shape of the "Juan Gris" piece, the use of the basic square shape, which is constitutive for all of Flavin's *icons*, seems to be an artistic instrument avoiding this artistic composition since the fixation of the side lengths determines the structure of the work as a whole. The pedantic documentation of the exact description of the different types of lamps and color also indicates the artist's desire to qualify his personal, manual involvement in the creation of the works. In the way an icon painter follows certain patterns and instructions in creating images of icons, Flavin puts together a catalogue of characteristics for his *icons*, while he sees these detached from his own person. The positioning of the tubes on the *icons II–IV* and *VII* can clearly be traced back to discernible artistic decisions. Otherwise Flavin tries to be as objective as possible. The standard lengths of the fluorescent tubes determine the side lengths of the first three *icons*. Thus, after deciding on the square basic structure there is no further need for the artist to interfere compositionally. In *icon V*, the side length is exactly the length of seven lamp mountings and on the *icons* that hold a flashing light on the canted corners, the realization follows strict geometrical rules. The "non-handmade" status of the Russian icons is something one could also apply to Flavin's *icons*. He sees himself as a medium, as distanced and objectively descriptive as possible, who, according to a stringent brief within a tightly set framework completes variations on a pattern. The gestural characteristics of the "Juan Gris" piece are no longer recognizable.[49]

The most apparent distinction to the square "Juan Gris" work is the application of lamps. The connection of a square, box-like structure with a lamp is only to be found among the *icons* in Flavin's œuvre. The main thrust of the self-activating luminescence of the Russian icons, which are also often constructed in square shapes, clearly connects Flavin's *icons* and these traditional religious works. While the Russian icons glow in the light of a higher divine reality and testify to the presence of a sanctified person already liberated from his carnal existence, Flavin's lamplight catapults the viewer into everyday *jetztzeit*, as Benjamin termed it. The electrification of a still discernible form of picture by naked light bulbs, flashing lights and fluorescent tubes is not intended to conjure up sacredness but rather expresses an anchorage into the present. The artist seeks to create contemporary art by means of contemporary instruments. Nonetheless the reference to traditional icons is obvious: the self-activating luminescence of the religious works counts as one of the main characteristics and is essential for the phenomenon of *real presence*. Scientifically, the gold ground cannot of course generate active radiance; it can merely reflect the light it receives. Flavin's *icons* radiate from within not just because we feel they do or religious perception enables us to think they do. They do so unmistakably thanks to electrical power. In a way, Flavin has made the constant claim of classical religious works a reality through the luminescence of his *icons*. Their light may be "finite" (it is actual and does not have a spiritual origin), yet it is completely realistic in its profanity and in that sense not illusionist.

East New York Shrines

Flavin's exploration of the use and effect of Russian icons is documented in the detailed sketch dated December 12, 1962 (fig. 22). With the title "Iconostases", he summarizes different alternative draft proposals for his first four *icons*. The wall of the "Iconostases" in orthodox chapels separates the area open to the 'flock' from that of the priests.[50] In most cases the wall is covered in icons hung closely side by side, creating a patchwork of images. This was an inspiration for Flavin's reflection as presented here. In different combinations the *icons* are sketched directly next to one another, tipping sideways (bottom right) or they are placed above each other. The first two *icons*, for instance, are drawn with a 90-degree turn (top middle) and the third *icon* appears in a 180-degree turn.[51] The drawing is

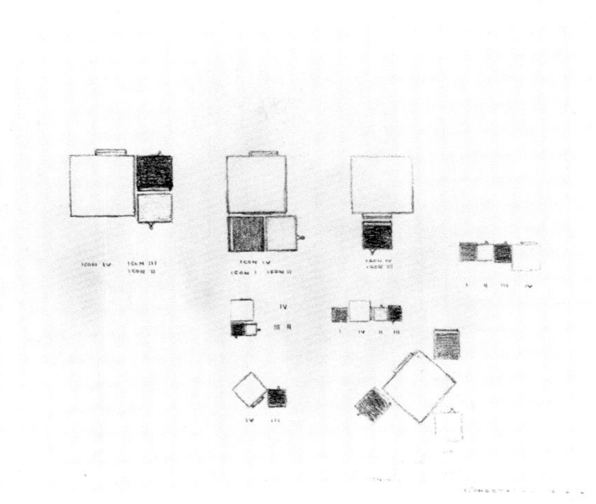

22 *iconostases (for icon I, II, III, and IV)*, 1962, pencil on paper, 11 x 13¹⁵⁄₁₆ in. (27.9 x 35.4 cm)

descriptive evidence of the way Flavin deals with the history of religious images: He consciously takes them up while transforming them at the same time. Yet, the sketches of tipped or twisted hangings indicate Flavin's extremely ambivalent attitude toward the Church and religion.

The artist himself wrote the following in his 1964/65 *autobiographical sketch*: "I used the word 'icon' as descriptive, not of a strictly religious object, but of one that is based on a hierarchical relationship of electric light over, under and against and with a square-fronted structure full of paint 'light'."[52] Here, Flavin tries to eliminate any religious aspect and reduces his idea of the *icon* to a combination of box-structure and electric light. Staving off religious convictions plays an important role in Flavin's life: His *autobiographical sketch* reveals how his father had intended Flavin and his twin brother to both pursue a career in the clergy, something the father had himself been denied. His father came from a pious Irish Catholic immigrant family. Flavin himself wrote: "Somehow, at eighteen, I began to think about art – Roman Catholic diversions of it, of course."[53] After attending a Catholic high school to prepare him for a seminary, Flavin opposed his father's wishes. This protest against traditional religious beliefs also fascinated him as regards one of his most admired literary figures, namely James Joyce. The Irish author had rebelled fiercely against

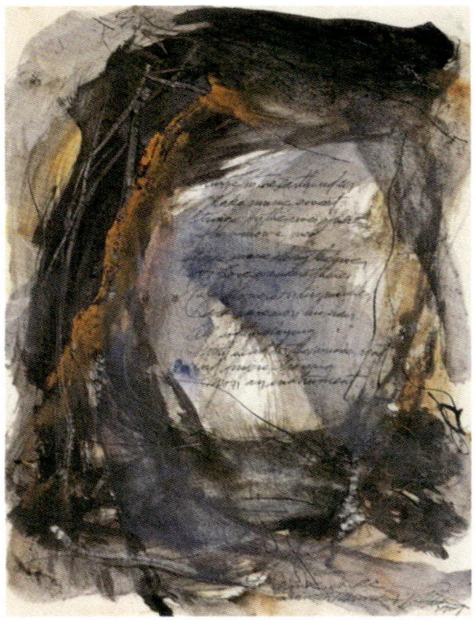

23 *Chamber Music I, no. 6 (to James Joyce)*, 1959, carbon ink, watercolor and charcoal on paper, $11\frac{15}{16}$ x 9 in. (30.4 x 23 cm)

his surroundings, which were steeped in Catholicism, and had turned away form his arranged education to become a priest.[54] Joyce appears in a few of Flavin's watercolor works as early as 1959. The artist had been inspired by Joyce's poems from the 1907 *Chamber Music* volume, which he transferred by hand onto his drawings (fig. 23) – one of his first dedications is to be read in the title of this work. His *autobiographical sketch* should also be seen in this light. With clear literary aspirations and conventionalized elements the then 32-year-old traced his family environment, his childhood and the years of his youth leading into adolescence in an endeavor to highlight the context in which he evolved as an artist. Clearly, he used Joyce's autobiographically influenced coming-of-age novel "A Portrait of the Artist as a Young Man" as an orientation.[55]

Religiousness and a conservative way of life are, in any case, themes that Flavin dealt with from an early childhood age on. With the *icons* he turns towards an area of Catholicism that is essential to the Russian Orthodox Church, whereas for the Roman Catholic branch of the Church, at least since the Renaissance, its symbolic meaning is limited. The balance between distance from and closeness to this tradition helps us understand his toying with the staunch features of the iconic images. On the one hand, the *icons* are an everlasting example of practiced faith that the artist opposed vehemently. On the other, these *icons* derive from a cultural region that cannot necessarily be equated with his own cultural background. The variations on the iconostases page (fig. 22), not to mention his earliest sketches (see fig. 4), reflect a certain attitude of distance and a felt neutral position as regards icons. Equally, the three-year inquiry into the opportunities for creating contemporary icons shows how important this topic was to the artist.

At the same time Flavin, together with his wife Sonja, worked on a group of works entitled "East New York Shrines" (fig. 24).[56] In 1962, he developed the shape of the works that were then to be completed through 1966. All in all, ten luminescent objects put together with a standard can and a porcelain bracket create kitschy illuminated light that reveals an image of the Virgin Mary.[57] On balance, these works are very handy objects (they are 11⅜ in. high) and can be situated in various places serving as little family altars. The message of these objects is unmistakable: not only does the artist raise fiercely kitschy lamps to the status of works of art, he also combines them ironically with a can of tomatoes, the brand name "Pope" printed on the label. This way the Virgin is enthroned above the nominal successor of her son, who was purportedly conceived immaculately. In this case the "Pope" does not refer to the Holy Father but to the producer of "whole, peeled tomatoes". Flavin confronts us with the question of appearance and reality or truthful belief and hypocritical piety.

"Ecstasy"

The process of May 25, 1963 is directly linked to this range of topics. After over two years of intense exploration and experimenting with artistic combinations of lamps and wooden boxes, Flavin disen-

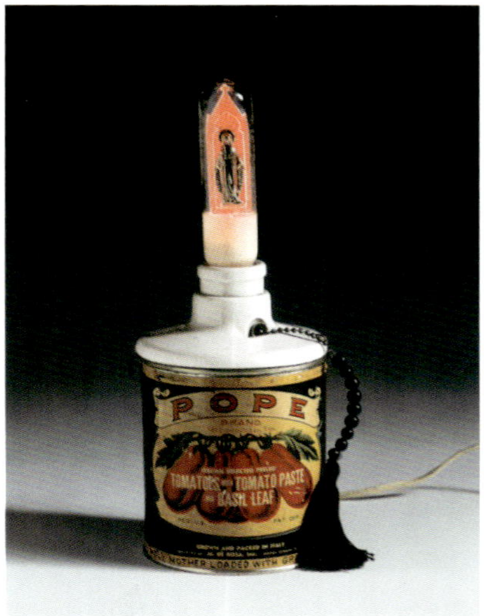

24 *East New York Shrine*, 1962–66, can, porcelain receptacle, pull chain, Aerolux bulb, black glass beads, 11⅜ in. (30 cm) high, 3½ in. (11.5 cm) diameter

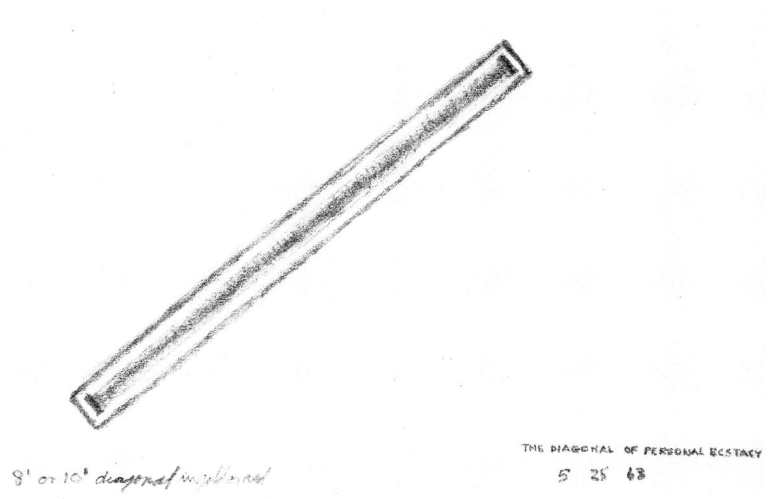

25 *the diagonal of personal ecstasy*, 1963, pencil on paper, 3 x 4 15/16 in. (7.6 x 12.5 cm)

gaged radically from this work method that was still connected to the classic formation of images. "From a recent diagram, I declared the diagonal of personal ecstasy (the diagonal of May 25, 1963), a common eight-foot strip with fluorescent light of any commercially available color. At first, I chose 'gold'," Flavin writes in his *autobiographical sketch*.[58] The drawing of the day (fig. 25) that symbolizes the first result of his mental break-through shows, to begin with, only gold and red as alternative colors. As with the first two *icons,* these two colors are the first to cross Flavin's mind. In this way he first implemented the idea of the golden tube that is attached to the wall precisely in a 45-degree angle (see p. 77).[59]

This stance was fundamental for the artists' further development. The realization of the importance of this act seemed to give him an intense sensation of emphasis. Anyhow, it is surprising that Flavin chose the expression "ecstasy", which spontaneously kindles religious associations and seems to contradict the strict visual appearance of the plain fluorescent tube that is connected to rationality rather than to the world of emotional perception. The Church describes ecstasy as the moment in which earthly and divine power meld or even as the joy of leaving the self and moving into the sphere of a higher being. Thus, it describes a process that is not accessible to the intellect. It is beyond our rational understanding. In the same manner as with the *icons* Flavin, in a second step, distances himself from the religious connotations of his work. Later he dedicates the *diagonal* to Constantin Brancusi and Robert Rosenblum and by changing the title to "the diagonal of May 25, 1963" eliminated the expression 'ecstasy'.[60] It seems that the proclamation of "personal ecstasy" appeared to him to be too spontaneously individual and a little too near to the connotation of the genius artist receiving inspiration from a divine, higher source.

Even though precisely this ambivalence is also noticeable in the *icons*, May 25, 1963 marks a turning point in Flavin's work. At first he appears to have moved the imaginary and material content of the *icons* into a further creative phase of work. Especially the color descriptions for the drawing (fig. 25) and the first layout in gold (see p. 77) can be seen as a continuation of the line of thought behind the icon theme. Yet he resolutely turns his back on this symbolic language during his first presentation of "the diagonal" in the Wadsworth Atheneum in 1964: There, he chose a daylight-white tube, dedicated it to Brancusi and titled the piece descriptively "the diagonal of May 25, 1963". Similarly he proceeded during his second presentation in the Kaymar Gallery (also in 1964): the fluorescent tube

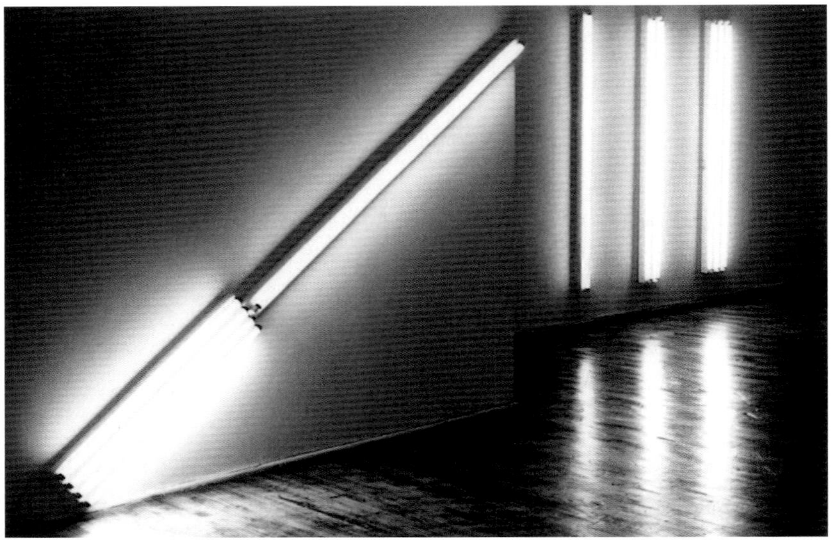

26 right: *the nominal three (to William of Ockham)*, 1963; left: *alternate diagonals of March 2, 1964 (to Don Judd)*, 1964. Installation view, Green Gallery, 1964

dedicated to Robert Rosenblum now has a cool-white color. The revised choice of color and the inscriptions and objective titles point up the momentous transition in Flavin's œuvre, something that was also to strongly influence his art thereafter.

In a 1972 interview Flavin talks about the method he maintains of dedicating his works:

> "The dedications are mostly extraneous but personal. They're sentimental, and that's nice. But they're apart. Occasionally, I've extended the dedication, and you can tell when I have. The dedication at the Jewish Museum, "to those who have been killed in ambushes", almost had inductive subject matter. There I almost had the literature and the installation in mind simultaneously; but that's very, very rare. I would say it's almost singular. Some people fret over the dedications. They should just let it go. It's a lovely, incidental thing. It's a very fine sentiment to me. It's the kind of trifling that makes life easier to take from time to time."[61]

While the dedications attest to an emotional element that runs through Flavin's entire œuvre, the titles of the *icons* express a subjectivity that the artist later reduced noticeably. They are precisely not an expression of some trivial pleasantness but are rather an integrated element of the works. These are "real" titles that give specific information about the artist as an individual. The concept of "ecstasy" also belongs into this category. With the change of the title of the *diagonal* something more than just naming his work took place. Dan Flavin takes another step back from the subjective naming of contents. Here, the title is meant to no longer hint at the artist's emotional world but rather describe a circumstance objectively.

The *diagonal* is equally telling evidence of the continuity in the relations of form and content within Flavin's œuvre. Geometrically speaking, it is the variable equivalent to the maximum length in any square form and a phenomenon that Flavin takes to the limits of defined space with his barriers as from 1968. On the other hand, it is a form that can hardly be experienced without being associated with its contents. It becomes apparent with the *icon VII (via crucis)* that he does create a connection to the contents of the piece.[62] Set free from the iconic square structure and attached to the bare wall, the luminescent *diagonal* evokes the old Christian tradition of images created to symbolize communication between the heavenly and earthly sphere.[63]

A comment from a Franciscan monk

The ambivalence between Flavin's quests for artworks free of reference and his actual creating is most visible in his 1963 pieces "The nominal three (to William of Ockham)" (see p. 74/75). Dan Flavin showed these in the New York Green Gallery in 1964 during his first exhibition exclusively displaying fluorescent tubes. The work consists of one fluorescent tube on the left, a set of two tubes in the middle, and a set of three tubes on the right, all of which colored in a cool-white. Flavin installed them as a sculpture on one of the walls in the gallery (fig. 26). All fluorescent tubes, eight feet long, were aligned vertically without touching the ground. The distance between each of the three objects ranged less than a meter. In his 1969 retrospective in Ottawa he placed the set of two tubes in the center of the wall, the single tube and the set of three on the outer edges of the wall. All tubes then touched the ground. The distance between each of the three sets ranged approximately four meters.

In a letter to Mel Bochner, dated November 1, 1966, Flavin wrote the following about Franciscan monk William of Ockham who was mentioned in his dedication:

> "I enclose a lovely tempering aphorism which has been with me for a few years. 'Entia non multiplicanda praeter necessitatem.' 'Principles (entities) should not be multiplied unnecessarily.' Of course it is 'Ockham's Razor'. (...) Briefly, my Columbia Viking Desk Encyclopedia recognizes William of Ockham thusly... 'd.c. 1349, English scholastic philosopher, a Franciscan. Embroiled in a general quarrel with Pope John XXII, he was imprisoned in Avignon but fled to the protection of Emperor Louis IV and supported him by attacking the temporal power of the papacy. Rejecting the doctrines of Thomas Aquinas he argued that reality exists solely in individual things and universals are merely abstract signs. This view led him to exclude questions such as the existence of God from intellectual knowledge, referring them to faith alone.'"[64]

William of Ockham's nominalist worldview demonstrates a theoretical thrust that developed within Medieval scholastic philosophy in opposition to universalism. The title "the nominal three" relates to William of Ockham just as much as the dedication of Flavin's work. The artist was fascinated by the pragmatic straightforwardness of Ockham's concept of reality[65] as well as by his notion of God. So it is all the more worthwhile to think about the change within the presentation of this work.

During 1963 and 1969 Flavin gradually developed his expansive works. While the original presentation showed the trivial procedure of counting "one, two, three" through an image-like object attached to a wall, the thereafter conventional triptych-like composition of the three objects now extended over an entire wall (see p. 72/73), referring to its expanse and making the installation of other works in the room impossible. It assumes a room-filling and defining scale. Even though Flavin's arrangement of the tubes toys with the idea of trinity (while present, this does not derive from the unitary concept of the "Holy Trinity" but, according to Ockham's theory, shows the actual triad of "one, two, three") the altered way of presentation consciously evokes a sacred pathos that could resemble the inside of a church, for instance the transept or apsis. What emerges here is that this work, while inwardly dealing with the concept of trinity and Ockham's belief and idea of reality, changes not only in form but also in content solely thanks to the modified installation. This creates an atmosphere of celebration in the room, generating a contemplative space that channels the spiritual aspect of the work, making it apparent to the viewer. Thus, Flavin's mastery of his craft is complete: The bare structure of the room connects to the object-like tubes. The artificial light fills the space of the room and engages with the daylight entering from above. The profane banality of the "one, two, three" intermingles with questions of faith and God.

The Russian avant-garde and contemporary icons

It is hardly surprising that the opening question by Bruce Glaser in the legendary 1964 radio interview with Frank Stella, Donald Judd and Dan Flavin aimed at the link between the three artists and the works of Malevich and the Constructivists.[66] The convictions and artistic statements of the Russian avant-garde of the 1920s were very familiar to the New York artistic community at the beginning of the sixties.[67] Dan Flavin himself stated in 1965:

27 Andy Warhol, *Gold Marilyn Monroe*, 1962, acrylic, silkscreen ink, gold paint, and spray paint on linen, 83¼ x 57 in. (211.5 x 144.8 cm), The Museum of Modern Art, New York. Gift of Philip Johnson, 1962 (cat. rais. # 248)

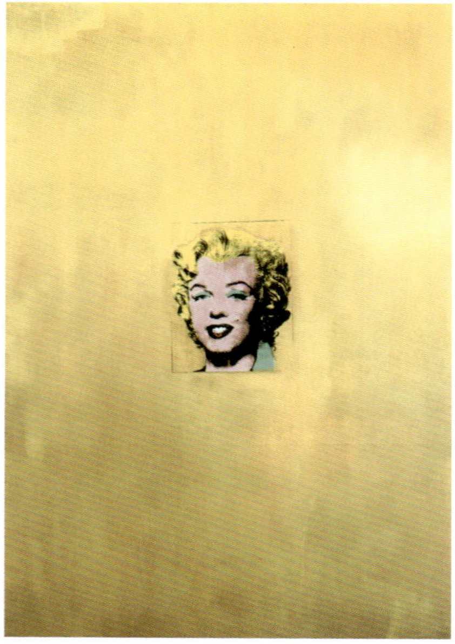

> "Thus far, I have made a considered attempt to poise silent electric light in crucial concert point to point, line by line and otherwise in the box that is a room. This dramatic decoration has been founded in the young tradition of a plastic revolution that gripped Russian art only forty years ago. My joy is to try to build from that 'incomplete' experience as I see fit.
>
> Monument 7 in cool white fluorescent light memorializes Vladimir Tatlin, the great revolutionary, who dreamed of art as science. It stands, a vibrantly aspiring order, in lieu of his last glider, which never left the ground."[68]

Quite naturally Flavin sees himself in line with the tradition of the Russian avant-garde artists. He wishes to mentally continue their yet incomplete project. It also seems only logical that he then referred to his large group of works titled "monuments for V. Tatlin" which he developed through into his late phase. Within his œuvre this is the clearest evidence for his conscious dialogue with the Russian artists of that time. His enthusiasm for Vladimir Tatlin is evident; yet his thoughts about Malevich's "Black Square" and his idea of a contemporary icon connected to the Orthodox tradition are not documented. What is however crucial is the fact that the historical and cultural conditions in Russia in the year of 1913 were very different to those of New York in 1961. So, the quest for the icon of the 20th century led to accordingly varied results.

Tatlin was a trained icon painter.[69] This alone explains the fundamentally different approach to the classic icon. The rejection of figuration and the purely abstract image derived from the strict scheme of the Orthodox icons that were ubiquitously known to all.[70] Furthermore, icons were still an important source of income for artists. Regarding Flavin, one should assume a conscious exploring. He noted in his diary that he deliberately searched for these sculptures during his visit to the Metropolitan Museum, but one cannot assume he had a common familiarity with the icons. A parallel of determined refusal of the European pictorial tradition likewise on the Russian and American side can be seen.[71] Both sides were equally fascinated by the phenomena of the *real presence*. The feature of "incorporation" that opposes the classic theme of representation, theoretically legitimates the giving of meaning to the purely formal sign language of the abstract images. While Malevich replaced religious content with a strict and penetrating Absolutist philosophy regarding the world's nature (which manifested itself in his writings on Suprematism) comparable symbolical systems are foreign to Dan Flavin's intentions. What thus clearly differentiates him from his Russian forefathers is his claim to create a piece of art freed completely of any form of ideology – a work that neither shoulders the excessive weight of European culture[72] nor a specific worldview.

It is to be assumed that Flavin's reference to the classic tradition of the icons already reflects the abstract adaptation of the Russian avant-garde – exemplary for this is Malevich's "Black Square". Nevertheless, his approach is independent and selective.

At this point it is worth taking a glance at another New York artist who was very well acquainted with the Orthodox tradition of the icons: Andy Warhol and his iconic portraits he created as from 1962.[73] The Marilyn Monroe series on a gold ground is especially interesting.[74] One of the first realizations of this type is a portrait-format rectangular version. It displays a large gold-colored surface in which a portrait of Marilyn Monroe is placed in the middle (fig. 27).[75] Warhol used screen-printing to place the portraits on the canvas. This enabled him to reproduce any photographic model (well-known media images) instantaneously and without any sort of manual interference. The silhouette character of the facial features is apparent in all versions of the "Marilyn Portraits", and all without exception were based on the same photo.[76] This gradual process that consists of transferring a found image onto a new medium that ultimately becomes a seemingly endless reproduction of the same image is reminiscent of the tradition of icon production. As well as the "non-handmade" image of the Orthodox Church it leans onto the predefined archetype that is merely copied and not created anew by the icon painter. Furthermore, Warhol emphasizes his procedure explicitly. After all, he intentionally reduced the quality of his photographic models during the preparation by screening and overexposing the photos. He did this to disclose the process of media translation.[77] Here, it was not his intention to show off his creative achievement and thus present his "artistic ego", as he instead calls for a dialog and a reflection on how images function. Marilyn's image is proverbially presented as a transfer image. The image is not a proxy of her personality but rather of her "persona" referring to the original Latin word for "mask", this being a comment on the function of the "Marilyn" image.

Warhol's extensive use of gold in combination with the formal arrangement of the picture gives the impression that the gold ground (in spite of the untypical proportions) frames the Marilyn portrait. This is remarkably similar to the making of classic icons where the indentation in the wooden base resembles the picture frame (see fig. 2). Another work in his series which consists of two tondi (fig. 28) and is usually termed a diptych demonstrates that Warhol's concept was a response to Marilyn Monroe's death. Both have a gold ground, one of them displays the black and white silkscreen of the Marilyn portrait and the other remained unprinted. This combination can be read as a commentary on the "Marilyn phenomenon": Her image in the media remains (something Warhol strongly helped happen) whereas her true self can no longer be fathomed in a personal encounter and remains as a blank space. In the unification of the two tondi, the private and unreachable image of the "real" Marilyn (which Warhol consequently presents as a blank space) encounters her image known throughout the world.

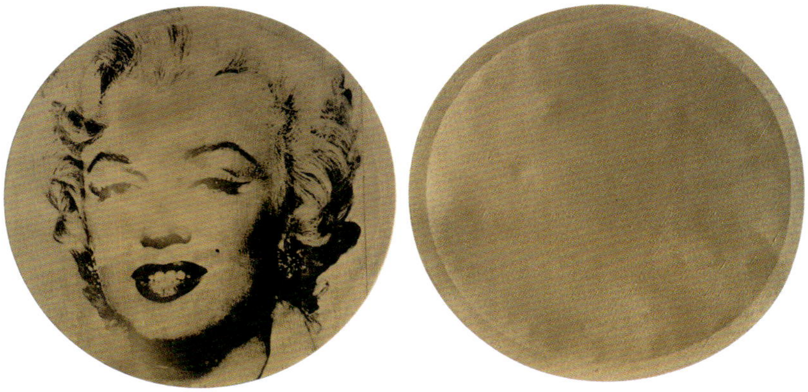

28 Andy Warhol, *Round Marilyn [Gold Marilyn]*, 1962, silkscreen ink and gold paint on two canvases, 18 in. (45.7 cm) each diameter, Froehlich Collection, Stuttgart (cat. rais. # 284)

Reflections of this type, dealing with death and the afterlife of the dead in memory, are characteristics that are found in both Warhol's and Flavin's works. Both men express their wish to commemorate certain persons abstractly and in very distinct ways. Warhol chooses the circular form for his Marilyn diptych and sets free the association of the cycle of nature. He confronts the theme of death, a symbol for the finite, with the idea of the infinite. This immediately precedes his large series of work "Death and Disaster". Flavin's "commemoration" utilizes electric light. He applies it in an iconic way: For technical reasons the service life of the fluorescent tubes is limited. Their "light of life" ceases after a certain period of time, contrasting sharply with the self-activating and everlasting charisma of the religious artworks. In the manner of modern "acheiropoieta" they proclaim new essential characteristics of art production in the early 1960s.

We have seen that Warhol likewise does not search for a direct dialog with the Russian avant-garde but is able to find his individual spin on the theme of the icon, revealing constants such as the gold ground and the conviction of the "non-hand-made" images.[78]

Significance and range of the *icons* in Flavin's œuvre

In the form of the eight *icons*, Dan Flavin laid the foundations for his later expansive works. The key features of traditional icons were the insistence on real presence, the intrinsic luminescence of the panels with their gold grounding, and the concept of the desubjectified creation of the images, that were not the result of an individual artist's genius. And these characteristics are reflected in a small group of Flavin's works. The transcendental eternal light of the Russian icons melds with the factual light of the fluorescent tubes. Flavin juxtaposes to a composition branded as European a contemporary model of "non-hand-made" art objects. The substantive references innate in the *icons* and very overt are decidedly abstract. Within Flavin's œuvre, the group of works is a halfway house between the very emotional, poetic assemblages of his early days and the cool fluorescent tube installations of his later years. At the same time, they reveal the transformational process in his artistic expression that formally speaking was henceforth highly stringent, and yet for all the abstraction nevertheless hinged on a complex matrix of sensory references.

A comparison of the approach taken by the Russian avant-garde in the 1920s with the representational concept of the classical icon shows that Flavin did not create his works in order to broach a dialog with that lineage. The icons fascinated him, their physically tangible presence inspired him to work conceptually on what were to be the maxims for his future work. Yet those original icons were not a direct point of reference for him, such as they had been for Tatlin and his colleagues. Andy Warhol's iconic portraits of the early 1960s give us an idea of how religiously influenced artists at this time intuitively responded to the concepts of classic icon painting and took this up in a contemporary vein in their art.

Dan Flavin's relationship to religion and faith must be a key issue in any discussion of his œuvre. And it is always linked to a very fundamental question as to the symbolic structures of his installations. The "East New York Shrines" he made at the same time as the *icons* show without doubt that Flavin was trenchantly cynical in his use of religious objects and thus set a critical distance between himself and the church. This method also attests to his stance as regards religion, and it was riddled with conflict. His identification with James Joyce also bears testimony to this. The *icons* are not a commentary on church and religion, however. What is decisive for Flavin is the concept and the immediate impact of the traditional icon as a form of art. Yet it would seem fair to assume that Flavin's religious family roots also formed a seedbed that was sensitive to the spiritual message of the classical images. We can discern a similar phenomenon in the works he made directly afterwards, such as the diagonals of May 25 and the piece dedicated to William of Ockham. Religious issues are always here in a subcutaneous form, their presence, albeit fissured, can be sensed there.

In the course of his critical inquiry into the icons, Dan Flavin dared to take the step into the world of three dimensions. The creative concept underlying the traditional icons, and their refusal to obey the key rules of perspective and representation, influenced his œuvre and caused his art to step out from the wall. In the midst of this inquiry into the icons he had the idea for his golden diagonals, and it grew on this fertile soil. Thus the link between the diagonals and the principles underlying the *icons* shows clearly that the intensive exploration on which he embarked for three years enabled him in 1963 to create a high amount of other fluorescent tube pieces in the footsteps of the incunabula. Although the output of the icon years was meager in quantitative terms, here Flavin laid the qualitative basis for his œuvre as a whole.

The tension between stringent facticity and symbolism in Flavin's art can perhaps be construed in the sense of the classical icons: They are not symbols, not representations of the respective saints, but imagine the real presence of that saint. Flavin's installations are not meant to refer to explicit issues, but are persuasive thanks to their factual, indeed their sheer presence. It is up to the viewer to enter into personal dialog with the artwork. There are no boundaries within Flavin's works and the viewer, meaning the art is immediately accessible. Physically one enters into a cone of light and is inevitably confronted with the interplay of (colored) artificial and natural light, and in the same breath one is confronted with the question of the relationship of technology and nature in everyday experience.

Notes

1 Letter from Flavin to Seymour H. Knox, President of the Albright-Knox Gallery, Buffalo, NY, of February 19, 1963, printed in: exhib. cat. "Dan Flavin", (Ottawa, 1969), p. 152.

2 "Leaving the picture behind" was an expression influenced by Laszlo Glozer following the exhibition "Western Art" (Westkunst), cf. exhib. cat. *Westkunst. Zeitgenössische Kunst seit 1939*, (Cologne, 1981), p. 234ff.

3 Haftmann, Werner: *Kasimir Malewitsch. Suprematismus – Die gegenstandslose Welt*, (Cologne, 1962), p. 19.

4 Linked to this is the question of Flavin's religiousness: Did he, as the son of a family of Irish emigrants, experience an upbringing which was closely connected to the Catholic Church?

5 The term "Minimal Art", which was implanted by art critics, found little love amongst the artists themselves. The original classification can be found in: Wollheim, Richard: "Minimal Art," in: *Arts Magazine*, January 1965, reprinted in: Battcock, Gregory: *Minimal Art. A Critical Anthology*, (Berkeley, Los Angeles & London, 1995; 1968), pp. 387–99.

6 This relates to an issue which is frequently discussed in connection with Minimal art – mostly by art critics. Michael Fried laid the foundations for the debate with his finding on "theatricality" in 1967. He asserted that minimalist artists – in spite of their declarations – were bringing a focus on content back into their works through the back door by using anthropological measures and the associations that the works provoke for the viewer. While Robert Morris was the only one of these artists who greeted a phenomenological reading of his works with audience participation, Donald Judd, for example, defended himself emphatically against this interpretation. Below we shall study Flavin's works free of this historical debate and examine the effect they have and the basic conditions of their creation. Some inspiring stations for the following publications were: Didi-Huberman, Georges: *Was wir sehen blickt uns an. Zur Metapsychologie des Bildes*, (Munich, 1999); and Zaugg, Rémy: *Die List der Unschuld: Das Wahrnehmen einer Skulptur*, (Eindhoven, 1980). The texts concerning the historical debate are printed in: Stemmrich, Gregor (ed.): *Minimal Art. Eine kritische Retrospektive*, (Dresden, 1995). This book also includes Hal Foster's "The Crux of Minimalism". Valuable documents can also be found in James Meyer's *Minimalism*, (London, 2000). For an overview of research literature on Minimal art see Neuner, Stefan: review of James Meyer: *Minimalism: Art and Polemics in the Sixties*, (New Haven, 2001), in: *Zeitschrift für Kunstgeschichte*, 67/2004, pp. 564–590. A comprehensive overview of literature and exhibitions concerning Minimal art is offered in exhib. cat. *A Minimal Future? Art as Oject 1958–1968*, (Museum of Contemporary Art, Los Angeles, 2004). The most comprehensive study of Dan Flavin's *icons* so far can be found in the following essay: Govan, Michael: "Irony and Light," in: Govan, Michael & Tiffany Bell: *Dan Flavin: the complete lights, 1961–1996*, (New Haven, etc., 2004), pp. 19–107, p. 23ff.

7 Psellos, Michael, "Treatise on an Icon of the Crucifixion (11th century)" in: Belting, Hans: *Bild und Kult. Eine Geschichte des Bildes vor dem Zeitalter der Kunst*, (Munich, 1990), p. 587f. (Likeness and Presence: A History of the Image before the Era of Art)

8 Just as on earth Christ was both the image and the incarnation of the original image of God the Father, without, however, differing from God in essence (the doctrine of the Holy Trinity), an icon is also identical in essence to the saint it depicts. Cf.: Krieger, Verena: *Von der Ikone zur Utopie. Kunstkonzepte der russischen Avantgarde*, (Cologne, 1997), p. 50ff.; Krieger, Verena: "'Wir suchen andere Werte, eine andere Inspiration, eine andere Kunst…'. Das Interesse der Avantgarde am Bildkonzept der Ikone," in: exhib. cat. *Chagall, Kandinsky, Malewitsch und die russische Avantgarde*, (Hamburg, 1998), pp. 31–40; Krieger, Verena: "Bildmittel der Ikone in Kunstwerken der Avantgarde – ein Überblick," in: exhib. cat. *Als Chagall das Fliegen lernte*, (Frankfurt/M., 2004), pp. 130–136.

9 See Belting (1990), p. 64ff.

10 For more information on the Abgar legend of the Mandylion see ibid., p. 236f.: "The oldest specimens of these privileged images come from the 6th century. The foremost of these is the Holy Mandylion, or the cloth imprinted with the image of Christ's portrait, which the town of Edessa in northern Syria saved from the Persians. In the Middle Ages it was kept in Constantinople as a palladium of the empire. The Veronica in St. Peter's Basilica in Rome, which is founded on a similar legend, supposedly surpasses the Mandylion." Ibid., p. 66. For information on the various legends see Dobschütz, Ernst von: *Christusbilder. Untersuchungen zur*

christlichen Legende (*Texte und Untersuchungen zur Geschichte der altchristlichen Literatur*, N.F.3), (Leipzig, 1899).

[11] Both legends are described in the Legenda Aurea, see Jacobus de Voragine: *Legenda Aurea* (1275), translated by Richard Benz, (Heidelberg, 1979), p. 814f. and p. 269f.

[12] Helmut Fischer writes in this regard: "Initially, icons are characterized by the gold ground (...) Gold is neither a color, nor does it represent one. We perceive color where light falls from this world onto the things of the world. By contrast, gold represents light itself, it is light from within light. Put differently: Gold is the glow on earth of the divine light that has no origin and of eternity in which there is neither time nor space. What emerges from the gold ground emerges from the glowing light of God, it is the light of the light without origin, and it shines into our tangible world, changing this and us." Fischer, Helmut: *Die Welt der Ikonen*, (Frankfurt/M., 1996), p. 21.

[13] See on this the exhaustive discussion in Belting, Hans: *Das echte Bild*, (Munich, 2006).

[14] Exhib. cat. *Three Installations in Fluorescent Light*, (Kunsthalle & Wallraff-Richartz Museum Cologne, 1973; Cologne 1973), p. 83

[15] Written communication from Peter Barnet, curator for Medieval art at the Metropolitan Museum of Art in New York, July 11, 2006.

[16] It should be noted that all electrical work for the icons was done by Sonja Flavin, the artist's wife at the time. See Govan & Bell (2004), p. 211

[17] In the last three *icons* the paint was, by contrast, applied directly onto the fiberboard.

[18] See Govan & Bell (2004), p. 211.

[19] This Flavin claim is quoted from Gibson, Michael: "The Strange Case of the Fluorescent Tube," *Art International*, 1 (fall, 1987), p. 105.

[20] The sketchbooks are in the possession of the artist's son, Stephen Flavin.

[21] Yet it is telling that none of the *icons* devised after May 25, 1963 were actually realized. Flavin dedicated all his efforts to the new approach offered by simply using fluorescent tubes on their own.

[22] Exhibition cat. (Ottawa, 1969), p. 122. The extremely precise information is made by Dan Flavin himself.

[23] See Flavin's comment in his "autobiographical sketch", exhib. cat. (Cologne 1973), p. 86.

[24] Govan & Bell (2004), p. 211.

[25] Compare works such as "Thomas Aquinas Doctor of Canon Law" (1959), "IN MEMORIAM ALBERT URBAN" (1959), "Apollinaire wounded (to Ward Jackson)" (1959–60), "mira mira (to Mrs. Brody)" (1960), "Africa (to seventy-two negroes)" (1960) and "Chamber Music I, no. 6 (to James Joyce)" (1959) (fig. 23). The works are shown in: exhib. cat. Ottawa (1969), p. 65; 79; 87; 89; 107.

[26] The first two icons differ from the subsequent ones in the composition of the titles – Flavin himself gave them in the form of labels stuck on the rear sides. The first line contains the expressions "the heart" and "the mystery", with the epithet "icon I" and "icon II" in brackets below. In other words, in contrast with the current style, title and subtitle are swapped around. As such great significance would seem to attach to the title epithets "the heart" and "the mystery" which only occur in these two cases in Flavin's light installations – especially the first two. For the full text of the labels consult Govan & Bell (2004), p. 211.

[27] Govan & Bell (2004), p. 215. Flavin wrote the following in his autobiographical sketch: "From a recent diagram, I declared the diagonal of personal ecstasy (the diagonal of May 25, 1963), a common eight-foot strip with fluorescent light of any commercially available color. At first, I chose 'gold'." Exhib. cat. Cologne, (1973), p. 87.

[28] Information is provided once again by Flavin's hand-written entry on the rear: the first line reads "ICON III (BLOOD)" and below, separated by an en-dash but without brackets "THE BLOOD OF A MARTYR". The final entry is not to be read as part of the title in its own right but in the sense of providing more information about "blood". Written on the rear label. Govan & Bell (2004), p. 212.

[29] Ibid., p. 212.

[30] There is no clear evidence of what the 1962 version of the work looked like. According to Sonja Flavin (conversation, Oct. 10, 2007), we can assume that the first version was more manual in appearance, and that quite possibly different material was used. The reverse of the work most certainly differed strikingly from the other *icons*. Highly geared to practical and swift production, the five Formica parts are joined together at the edges by straightforward strips, contrasting totally with Flavin's elaborate construction method with pinewood cross beams. Flavin's approval several years later for a reproduction of the work not then made by him reflects the continuous change in his method of working throughout the 1960s. He increasingly gave up actually producing his works (in the case of the fluorescent tubes the cabling for the installations etc.).

[31] In the initial version the artist had even used a cool white fluorescent tube, but found it too lacking in contrast from the corpus. "At first Flavin chose cool white fluorescent light for *icon IV*, but when he noticed that it combined too similarly with the color of the slick white plastic front, he switched to daylight for slight contrast." Exhib. cat. Ottawa (1969), p. 142.

[32] We would like to explicitly emphasize here that the descriptions refer to the second version of the work. It is possible that the original version did not use Formica sections but was made in a manner similar to the other seven icons. There is no option here other than to refer to the second version of the work made in 1969 and authorized by Dan Flavin.

[33] Exhib. cat. Ottawa (1969), p. 142.

[34] David John Flavin died of polio on October 8, 1962 after being ill for several years. Govan & Bell (2004), p. 183.

[35] Ibid., p. 142.

[36] A letter to Seymour H. Knox, President of Albright-Knox Gallery, Buffalo, NY, dated February 19, 1963, printed in: exhib. cat. Ottawa (1969), p. 152.

[37] Flavin planned to produce this work in memory of the 1916 Easter Uprising, in which Irish resistance fighters in Dublin were killed by British soldiers. The bulbs were to emit red light. Exhib. cat. Ottawa (1969), p. 160.

[38] Exhib. cat. St. Louis (1973), p. 10.

[39] In the course of it being exhibited, the work has also been presented as a mirror image, i.e., with the tube on the right side. The label Dan Flavin made for the back of the icon describes the tube as in the illustration of it here, namely as being on the left. Our special thanks for this information goes to Tiffany Bell, New York.

[40] "Dan Flavin, Donald Judd, Frank Stella. New Nihilism or New Art? Interview with Bruce Glaser" (1964), in: Meyer, James: *Minimalism*, (London, 2005) (2000), pp. 197–201, here p. 198. See, too, Judd's review of the Black, White and Gray exhibition in Wadsworth Atheneum in Hartford, Connecticut, March 1964, in which he writes of Flavin's *diagonal of May 25, 1963*: "There is some relation to the diagonals of Morris Louis." Judd, Don: *Complete Writings 1959–75*, (Halifax & New York, 1975), p. 119.

[41] A short text that deals with this drawing and that was revised by Flavin himself reads: "It may be that the fluorescent tube was meant to be yellow, the incandescent bulbs red and the masonite green." In: exhib. cat. *Drawings and Diagrams 1963–1972 by Dan Flavin*, (The St. Louis Art Museum, 1973), p. 18.

[42] In this context see the essay: Govan, Michael, "Sacred and Profane," in: Cooke, Lynne & Karen Kelly (eds.): *Robert Lehman Lectures on Contemporary Art*, (New York, 2004), pp. 181–93.

[43] Flavin also thought about using rotating lights. Next to his draft (fig. 15) for a version of this sort he wrote: "as it turns it destroys the square which I have been dealing with for the past year". However, he subsequently desisted from realizing this concept, which seemed to totally destroy the square pattern. Exhib. cat. Ottawa (1969), p. 146.

[44] Ibid., p. 178.

[45] This observation references Donald Judd's problematic claim that the new 3D works of art by so-called Minimalist artists should be "seen at once" ("singleness"), a claim that can only be maintained by splitting the act of perception into recognition (of the shape) at first glance and a procedural appreciation of the work over time. The extent of what the works have to say cannot be conveyed with a single glance. See Judd, Don: "Specific Objects," in: *Arts Yearbook*, 8, 1965, reprinted in: *Judd* 1975, pp. 181–189, here p. 182f. In this context see, too, the detailed analysis of the method of perception of a work by Donald Judd: Zaugg (1980). See, too, Didi-Huberman's fundamental survey in: Didi-Huberman (1999).

[46] According to a statement by the artist, see exhib. cat. Ottawa (1969), p. 108.

[47] Even though the stroke of the brush is revealed when eyed closely, from a distance they seem like prefabricated mass products. On encounter they require detailed attention, and only at second glance reveal their hand-made origin.

[48] Meyer (2005), p. 198.

[49] Surprisingly enough the critics' reaction to the first exhibitions presenting the *icons* hardly refer to this step and none mentions the connection to classic icons (the most significant exhibition took place from March 31 to April 14, 1964 in the New York Kaymar Gallery (fig. 20)). Flavin's work is described rather generally with expressions such as "romantic" – with a pejorative undertone. See Levin, Kim, "Reviews and Previews. New Names this Month," in: *ArtNews*, vol. 63, no. 1, (March, 1964), p. 14, reprinted in: *It is what it is. Writings on Dan Flavin since 1964*, Paula Feldman & Karsten Schubert (eds.), (London, 2004), p. 18. This expression appeared again in connection with a later exhibition in the Green Gallery (1964), Johnston, Jill: "Reviews and Previews. New Names this Month," in: *ArtNews*, vol. 63, no. 9, (January, 1965), p. 13, reprinted in: Feldman & Karsten (2004), p. 26. Also the inclusion of lamps in his works finds surprisingly little response. Apart from this, a 1964 review by Donald Judd on Flavin's exhibition in the Kaymar Gallery is of great interest. Here, for the first time all *icons* (apart from *icon IV*) were put out on display. Despite the fact that Judd explicitly writes about several of the *icons* and the underlying tone of his article is positive he seems to offer clear criticism of his friend Flavin. He described the works without once using the title "icon". Judd was fascinated by the clear objectivity of the pieces. At the same time he was not able to praise Flavin's link to the Classical tradition and the symbolical exaggeration that came with it. Judd, Donald: "New York Exhibitions: In the Galleries," in: *Arts Magazine*, 38, no. 7 (April), p. 31, reprinted in: Judd (1975), p. 124.

[50] On the process and history of the iconostasis see Belting, Hans: *Bild und Kult. Eine Geschichte des Bildes vor dem Zeitalter der Kunst*, (Munich, 1990), p. 253.

[51] This form of presentation for the third *icon* was chosen for the hanging by Donald Judd in the latter's house at Spring Street. Govan & Bell (2004), p. 212.

[52] Flavin, Dan: ...in daylight or cool white, in: exhib. cat. Cologne (1973), pp. 84–88, here p. 88.

[53] Ibid., p. 85.

[54] This can be seen in his early autobiographical writings "Portrait of the Artist as a Young Man", and even more

clearly in the fragmentary precursor of this text: "Stephen Hero". Sonja and Dan Flavins' son, who was born July 7th 1964, was named Stephen after the literary figure.

55 See loc. cit. cf. also Michael Govan's observations on the Flavin – Joyce relation in: Govan (2004), p. 32f.

56 Flavin's work on the shrines took place while moving house from Manhatten to Williamsburg, Brooklyn. The title "East" refers, according to Sonja Flavin, to the point of origin in the East of New York. Information given by Sonja Flavin, October 10, 2007.

57 The first work was dedicated to Ed Plunkett. On this – like on all the following versions of the shrines – an inscription is written saying: "HOLY MOTHER LOADED WITH GRACE PLEASE HELP [Name of a friend or a buyer] SONJA AND DAN FLAVIN [Year of origin between 1962 and 1966]." One work stayed in Flavin's possession. It is dedicated to David, the late twin brother of Dan Flavin. Govan & Bell (2004), p. 214.

58 Exhib. cat. Cologne (1973), p. 87.

59 It took approx. six months to realize the conceptual sketches. Flavin created the *diagonal* in nine customary colors and with this completes the range of colors for all his later works: red, yellow, blue, green, pink, warm white, cool white, daylight and soft white. Only the ultraviolet tube is not yet installed here. At no point did Flavin use colors or tubes specifically produced for him.

60 The original golden version was dedicated to Brancusi and the cool white one to Robert Rosenblum. The artist did not dedicate the other versions to anyone. See Govan & Bell (2004), pp. 215–18.

61 Dan Flavin interviewed by Phyllis Tuchman, March 9, 1972, in: Govan & Bell (2004), pp. 193–4, here p. 194.

62 In a 1982 interview with Tiffany Bell Dan Flavin said: "I was against spiritual and psychological outlooks on art. And I guess I skirted symbolic usages from time to time. There's no need for it, but I think I did it earlier on, with the icons, for instance, after the fact. The facts of these constructions were more important than any language that was attached to them (...) I'm not saying there wasn't symbolic reference there. That's what I am saying, there is. But sometimes the literature got to be a burden." Govan & Bell (2004), p. 196. Here also, 20 years after the creation of the works, the conflicting view on the symbolical exaggeration of the works becomes apparent.

63 See here the diagonal schemata of composition, especially of the Ascension or the Annunciation in the Western tradition. Also see actual artistic realizations of the moment of ecstasy as in Bernini's Holy Theresa of Avila in the Cornaro chapel in S. Maria della Vittoria in Rome. Also the dedication to Constantin Brancusi, the quintessence of whose work Flavin felt was the "Endless Column", fits here. His colleague and contemporary Carl Andre vividly shows this: "Brancusi for me is the great connecting piece into the earth, and the 'endless column' is, of course, the absolute climax of this experience. The sculptures reach up high and press down into the earth with a verticality that has no boundary. " Interview with Phyllis Tuchman, first published in: *Artforum*, vol. 8, no. 6, (June 1970), pp. 55–61, here as reprinted in: exhib. cat. *Carl Andre Sculptor 1996*, (Krefeld & Wolfsburg, 1996), pp. 40–5, here p. 45.

64 Exhib. cat. Ottawa (1969), pp. 204–6.

65 Flavin thus noted on this work on August 8, 1963 in one of his notebooks: "With *the nominal three* I will exult primary figures and their dimensions. Here will be the basic counting marks (primitive abstractions) restated long in the daylight glow of common fluorescent tubes. Such an elemental system becomes possible (ironic) from the context of my previous work." Quoted from exh. cat. Cologne (1973), p. 83.

66 Meyer, 2005 (2001), p. 197. Glaser also explored the relationship to the New Sculpture and the Purists. Stella and Judd stated that they in general did not see themselves in the lineage of European forms of abstract art. In the interview, Flavin does not take a stance on the issue.

67 Camilla Gray's broad study of the Russian art of the 1920s was published in 1962 and was noted by many artists at the time. Gray, Camilla: *The Great Experiment: Russian Art: 1863–1922.* Hal Foster states that Flavin's purchase of this book is recorded in his notebooks on August 21, 1962. Foster, Hal: "Dan Flavin and the Catastrophe of Minimalism," in: Weiss, Jeffrey (ed.): *Dan Flavin. New Light*, (New Haven, 2006), pp. 133–151, here p. 139. See also the following analyses of the relation of 1960's art to the Russian avant-garde: Foster, Hal: "Some Uses and Abuses of Russian Constructivism," in: exhib. cat. *Art into Life*, (Seattle, 1990), pp. 241–53, esp. p. 248; Tuchman, Maurice: "The Russian Avant-Garde and the Contemporary Artist," in: exhib. cat. *Avant-garde in Russia 1910–1930*, (Los Angeles County Museum of Art, 1980), pp. 118–21. See also Judd's writings on his relation to Russian art: Judd, Donald: "Malevich: Independent Form, Color, Surface," in: *Judd*, 1975, pp. 211–5 and: "On Russian Art and its Relation to my Work," in: Judd, Donald: *Complete Writings 1975–86*, (Eindhoven, 1987), pp. 14–18.

68 Exhib. cat. Cologne (1973), p. 84. First published with the heading *The Artists Say* in the summer edition of 1965 in the magazine *Art Voices*.

69 Krieger (1998), p. 32.

70 Ibid., p. 32.

71 Ibid., p. 32; Meyer (2000) (Glaser-Interview), p. 197.

72 This formulation borrows from statements by Carl Andre. See the interview with Andre conducted by Phyllis Tuchman, first printed in: *Artforum*, vol. 8, no. 6 (June 1970), pp. 55–61, reprinted in: exh. cat. Krefeld (1996), pp. 40–45 (translated into German) and pp. 46–51 (in the original), here p. 43.

73 Andy Warhol's parents immigrated to the United States from "Mikova, a vil-

lage then on the border of the Austro-Hungarian Empire, now on the Slovakian border, with Ukraine. Both are members of the Ruthenian religious community, whose liturgy is close to that of the Russian Orthodox Church. The family's piety is a strong influence in Andrew's childhood." Dallmann, Antje: *Andy Warhol – A Chronology in America*, exhib. cat. *Andy Warhol Retrospective*, (Tate Modern, London, 2002; London 2002), pp. 287–305, here p. 287.

[74] In December 1962, Michael Fried wrote a review on the afore-mentioned images and stated: "Warhol's beautiful, vulgar, heart-breaking *icons* of Marilyn Monroe", Fried, Michael: "New York Letter," *Art International*, Dec. 20, 1962, p. 57. Also the realization of the pictures of Liz Taylor and Jackie O. are suited for this comparison. The Marilyn works show the earliest result of this idea.

[75] Frei, Georg & Neil Printz (ed.): *Warhol: the Andy Warhol Catalogue Raisonné 01. Paintings and Sculpture 1961–1963*, (London, 2002), p. 247.

[76] We can discern two silkscreen inks here. See ibid., p. 257ff.

[77] Lüthy, Michael: "Die scheinbare Wiederkehr der Repräsentation," in: exhib. cat. *Andy Warhol. Paintings 1960–1986*, (Kunstmuseum Luzern, 1995), p. 38.

[78] Warhol's factory was clad, as is generally known, with Billy Name's tinfoil and was painted in all possible areas with silver color. In Warhol's circle, it was termed the "silver factory". Warhol said the following in *POPism*: "it was the perfect time to think silver. Silver was the future, it was spacy – the astronauts wore silver suits – Shepard, Grissom, and Glenn had already been up in them, and their equipment was silver, too. And silver was also the past – The Silver Screen – Hollywood actresses photographed in silver sets. And maybe more than anything, silver was narcissism – mirrors were backed with silver." in: Warhol, Andy and Pat Hackett: *POPism. The Warhol Sixties*. New York, 1980, p. 83. This attests to the breadth in which Warhol pondered the worth of silver as a material. Utterances regarding gold as materials are not known, but it can be expected that Warhol was very aware of the specific connotation of the gold base in connection with classic icons. Also his early use of gold colors, partly imitated leaf gold should be mentioned. For instance in his series of work "A la recherche du shoe perdu" (Portfolio with 14 offset prints) from 1955 or in his book *In the Bottom of my Garden* (21 pages, erotic drawings) from 1955 as well as pen and ink drawings on gold base that Warhol showed in his third exhibition in the Bodley Gallery in Dec. 1957. Bastian, Heiner: "Rituals of Unfulfillable Individuality – The Whereabouts of Emotions, Part One." in: exhib. cat. London (2002), p. 19.

Plates

icon I

icon I (the heart) (to the light of Sean McGovern which blesses everyone), 1961–62
oil on cold gesso on Masonite and pine, and red fluorescent light
25⅛ x 25⅛ x 4⅝ in. (63.8 x 63.8 x 11.9 cm) excluding fixture and lamp;
approx. 29 in. (73.7 cm) high including fixture and lamp

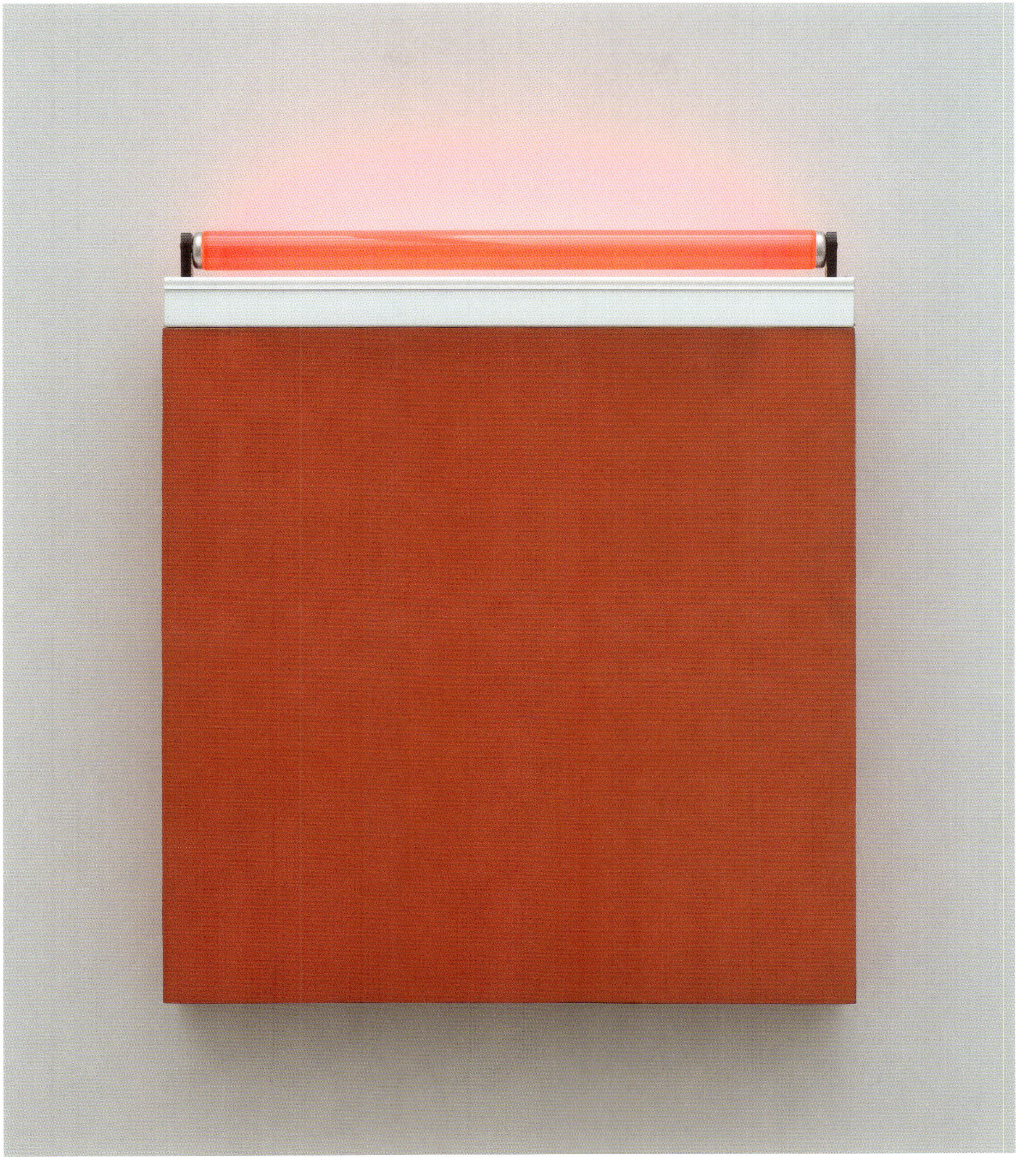

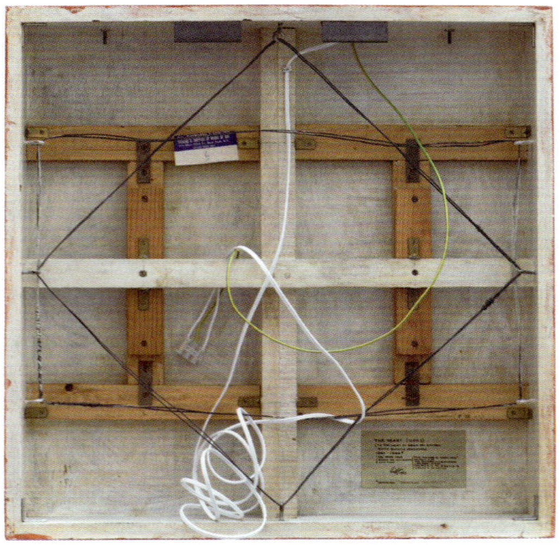

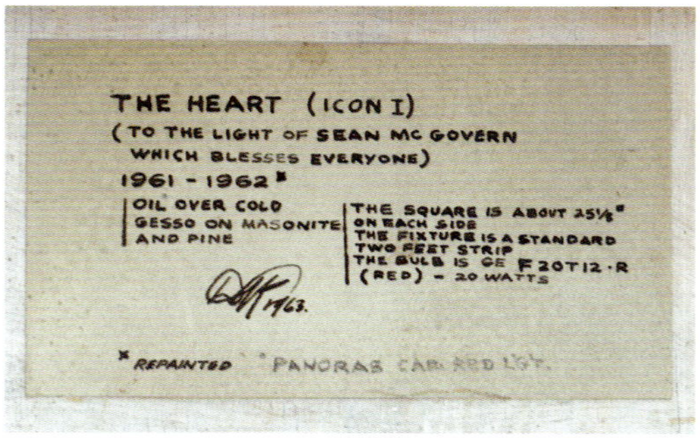
THE HEART (ICON I)
(TO THE LIGHT OF SEAN MC GOVERN
WHICH BLESSES EVERYONE)
1961 - 1962*
OIL OVER COLD
GESSO ON MASONITE
AND PINE
THE SQUARE IS ABOUT 25⅛"
ON EACH SIDE
THE FIXTURE IS A STANDARD
TWO FEET STRIP
THE BULB IS GE F20T12·R
(RED) - 20 WATTS
1963.
*REPAINTED

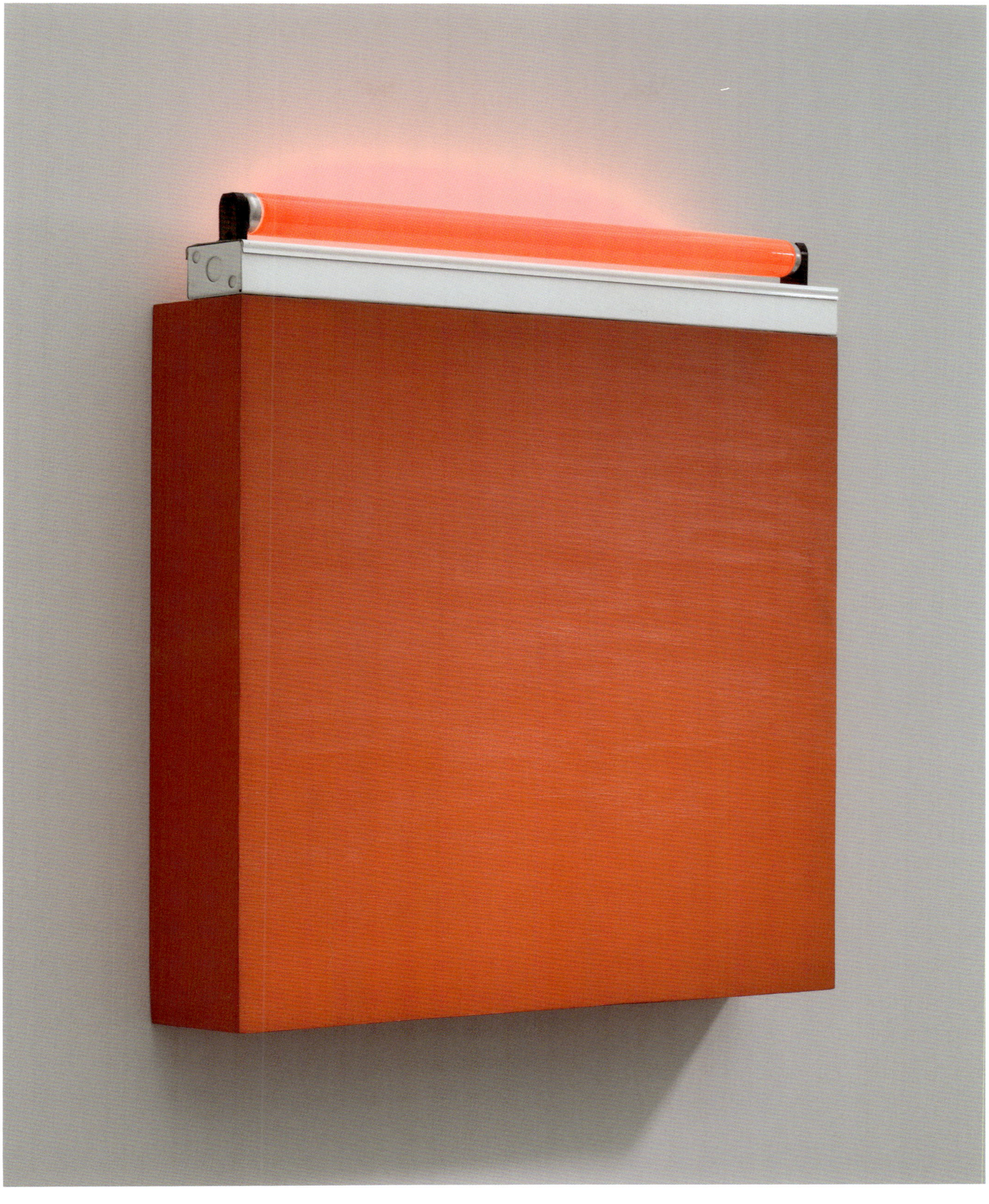

icon II

icon II (the mystery) (to John Reeves), 1961
oil on cold acrylic gesso on Masonite and pine, porcelain receptacle, pull chain, and amber "Firelogs Vacuum" incandescent bulb
25⅛ x 25⅛ x 4⅝ in. (63.8 x 63.8 x 11.9 cm) excluding fixture and lamp; approx. 30 in. high including fixture and lamp

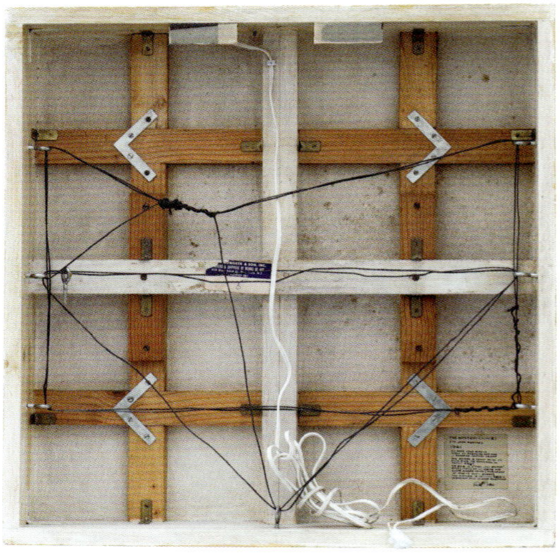

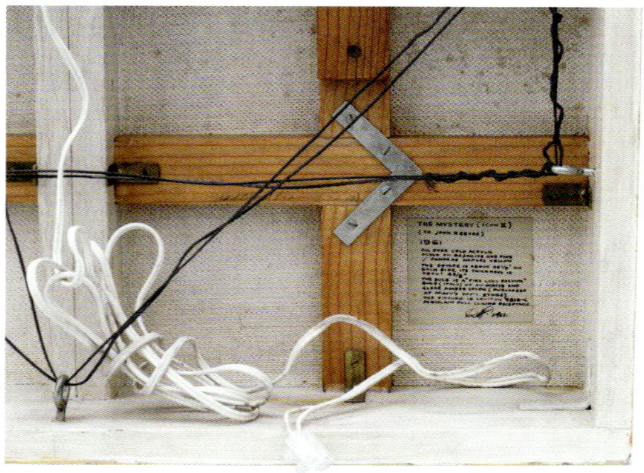

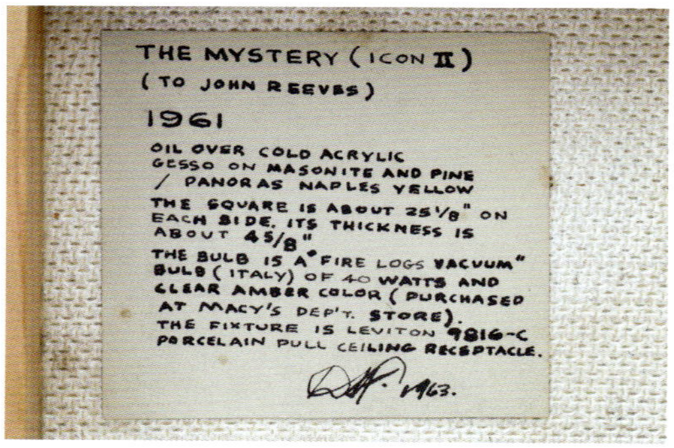
THE MYSTERY (ICON II)
(TO JOHN REEVES)
1961
OIL OVER COLD ACRYLIC
GESSO ON MASONITE AND PINE
/ PANORAS NAPLES YELLOW
THE SQUARE IS ABOUT 25 1/8" ON
EACH SIDE. ITS THICKNESS IS
ABOUT 4 5/8"
THE BULB IS A "FIRE LOGS VACUUM"
BULB (ITALY) OF 40 WATTS AND
CLEAR AMBER COLOR (PURCHASED
AT MACY'S DEP'T. STORE).
THE FIXTURE IS LEVITON 9816-C
PORCELAIN PULL CEILING RECEPTACLE.
1963.

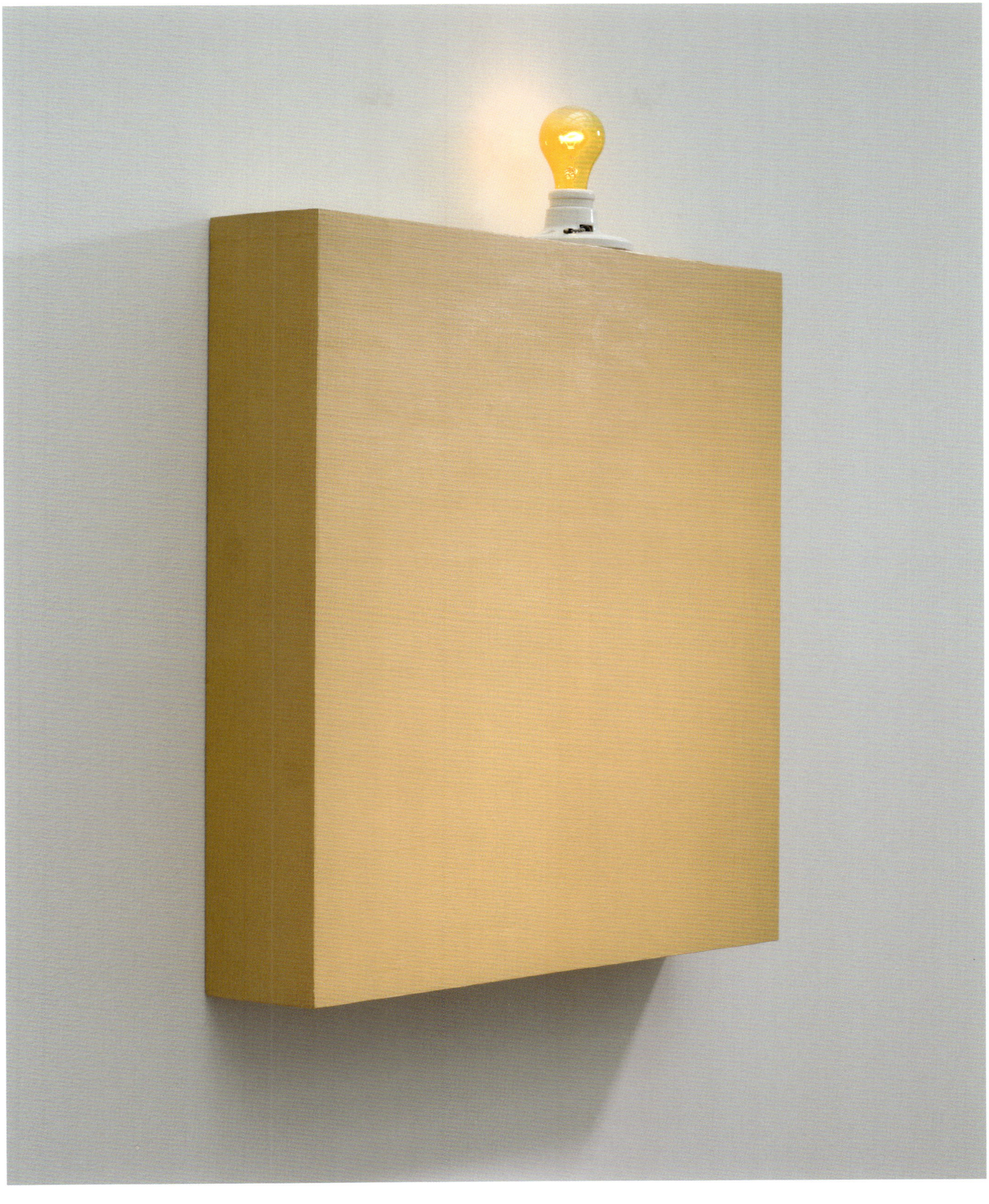

icon III

icon III (blood) (the blood of a martyr), 1962
oil and linoleum over cold acrylic gesso on Masonite and pine,
red incandescent light bulb, and red fluorescent light
25¼ x 25 x 5⅞ in. (64.1 x 63.5 x 14.9 cm) excluding fixtures and lamps;
approx. 34⅛ in. (86.7 cm) high including fixtures and lamps

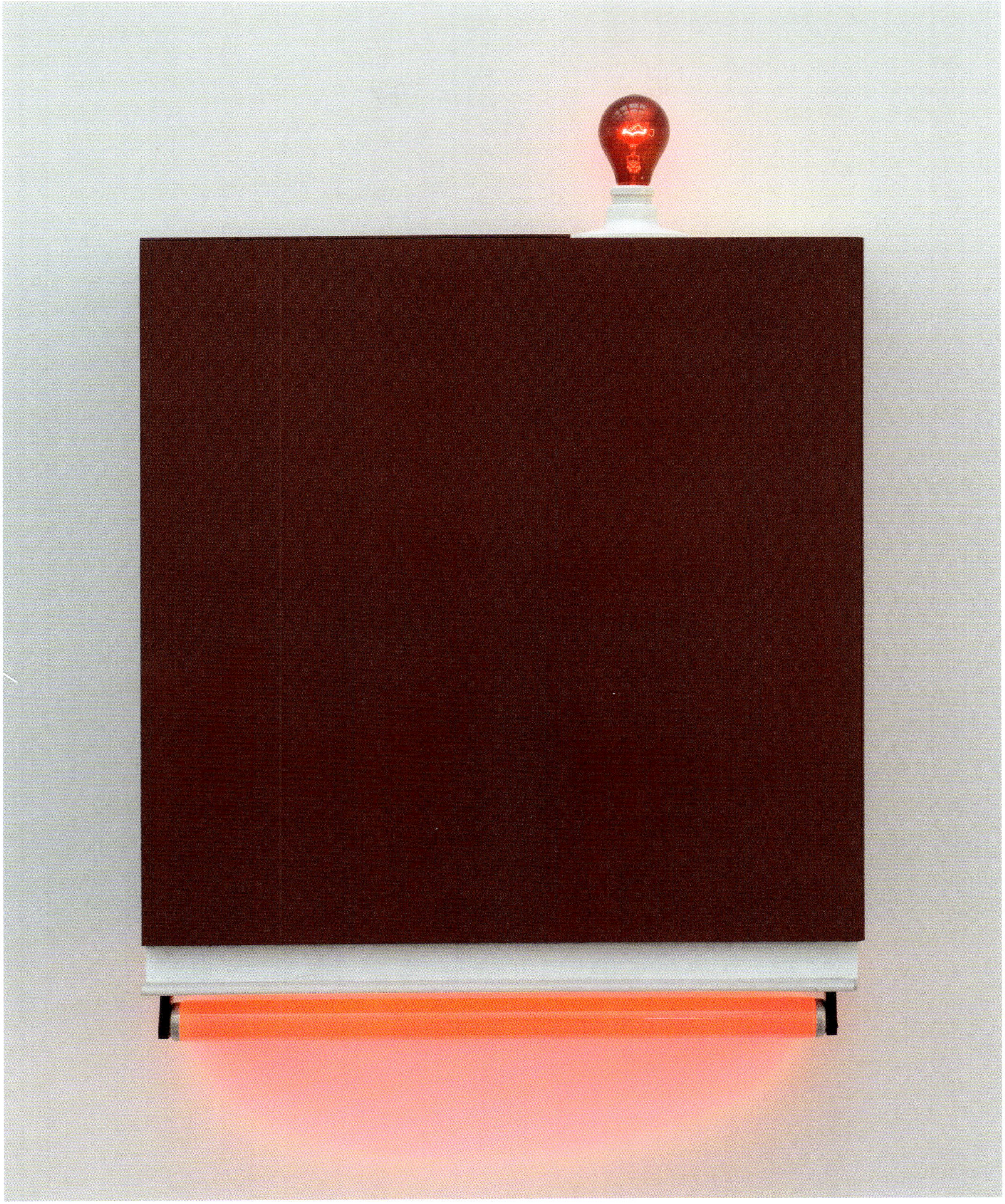

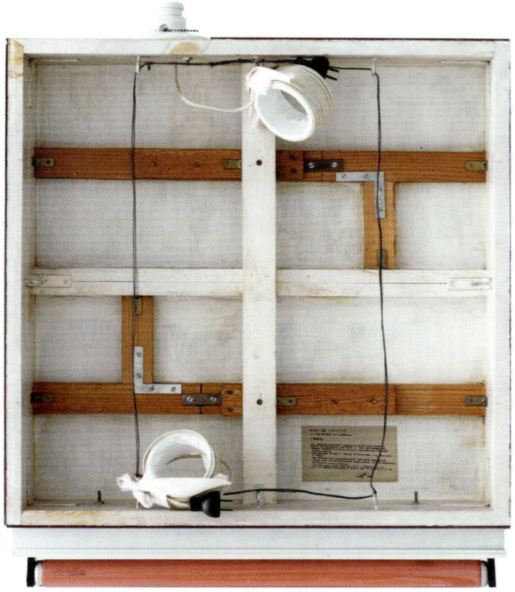

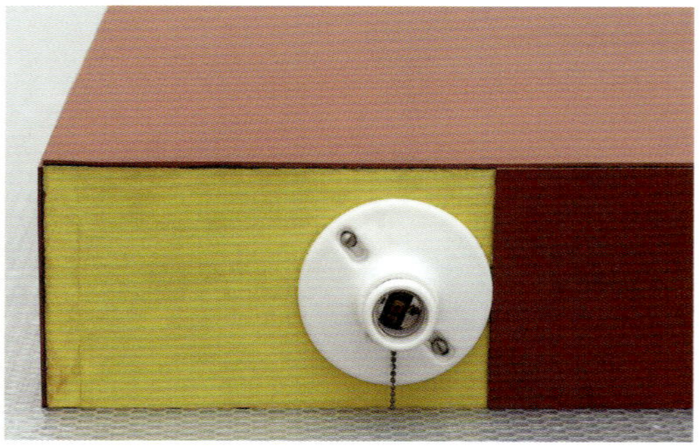

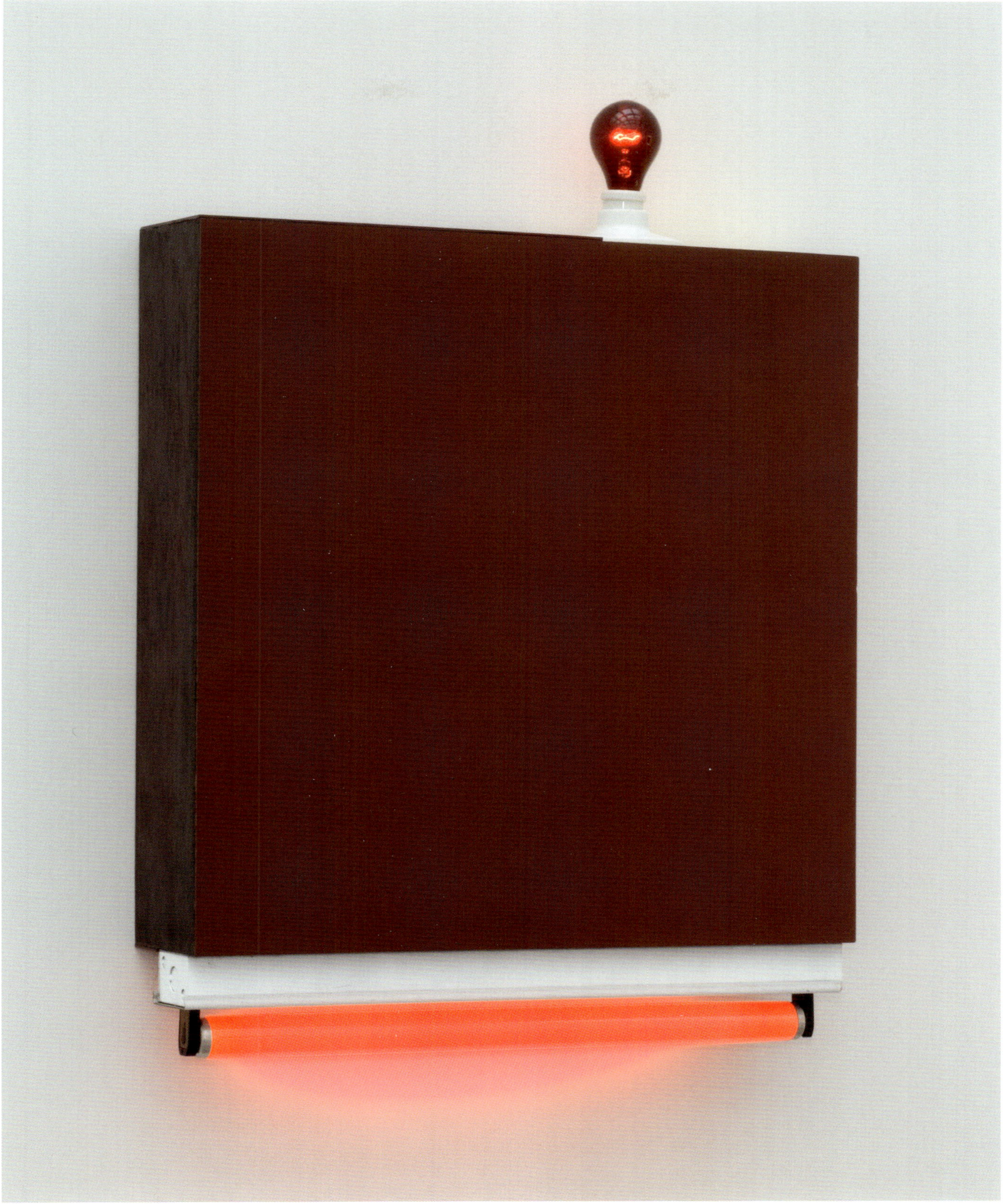

icon IV

icon IV (the pure land) (to David John Flavin [1933–1962]), 1962–69
Formica and daylight fluorescent light
44½ x 44½ x 11⅛ in. (113 x 113 x 28.6 cm) excluding fixture and lamp;
approx. 48⅜ in. (122.9 cm) high including fixture and lamp

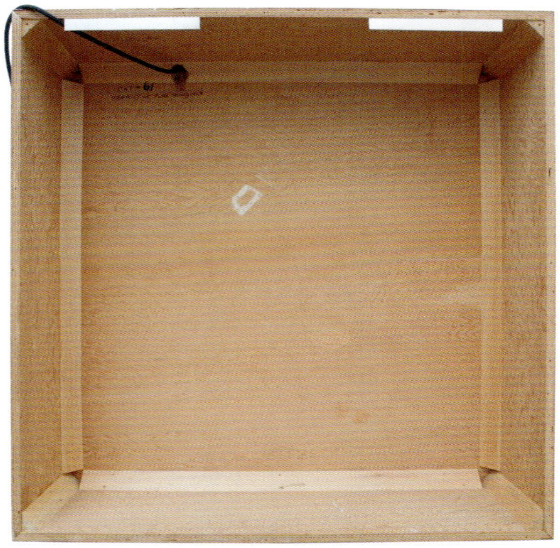

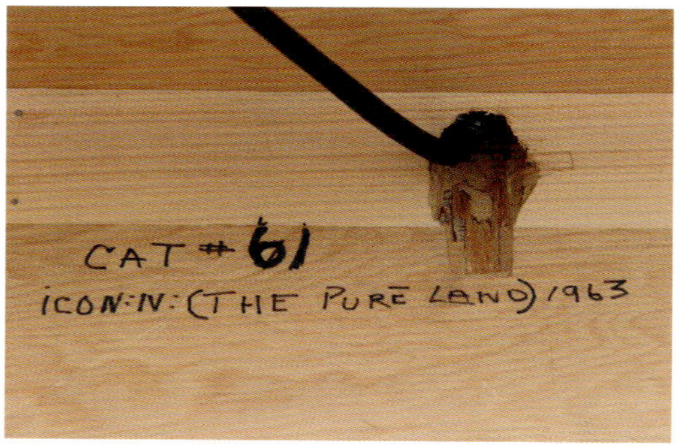
CAT # 61
ICON:N: (THE PURE LAND) 1963

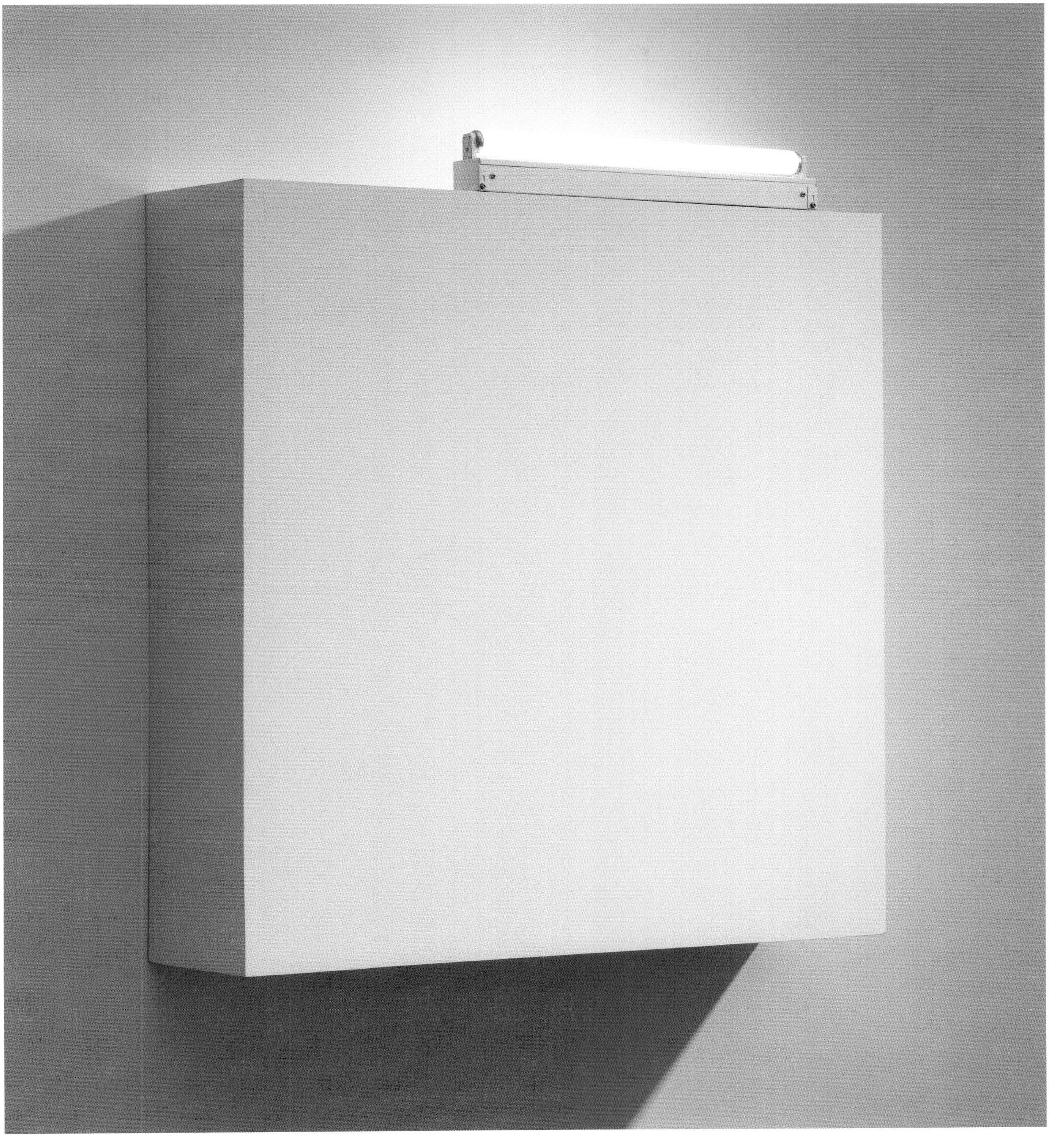

icon V

icon V (Coran's Broadway Flesh), 1962
oil on cold gesso on Masonite, porcelain receptacles,
pull chains, and clear incandescent "candle" bulbs
31⅝ x 31⅝ x 9⅞ in. (80.5 x 80.5 x 25.1 cm) excluding fixtures and lamps;
approx. 41⅝ x 41⅝ x 9⅞ in. (105.9 x 105.9 x 25.1 cm) including fixtures and lamps

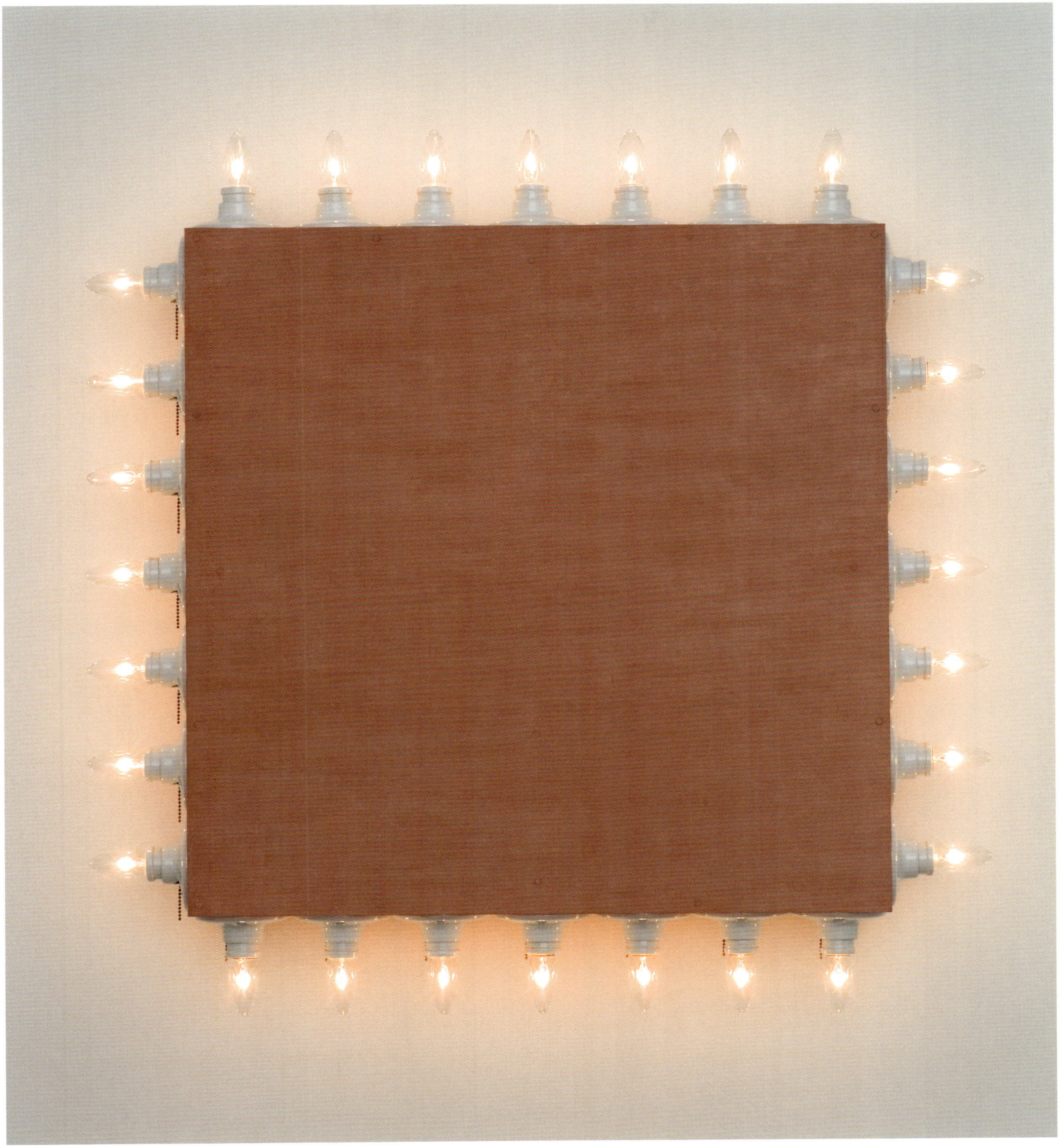

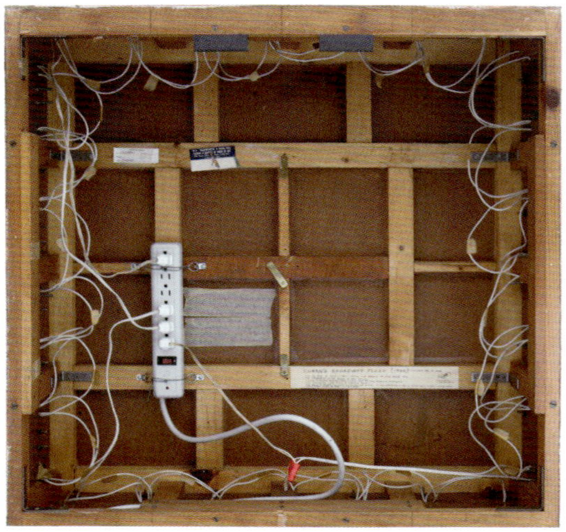

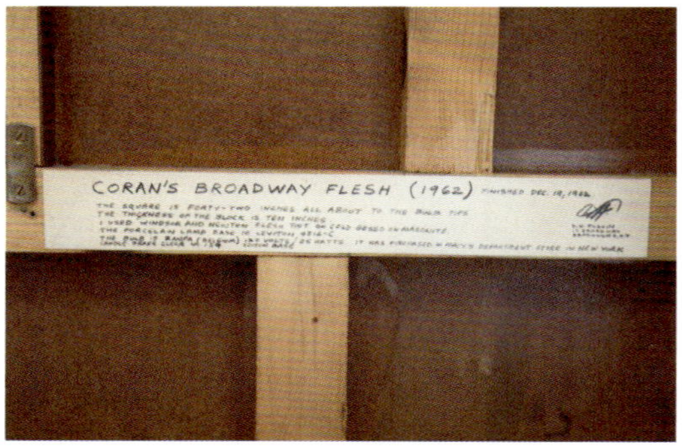
CORAN'S BROADWAY FLESH (1962)

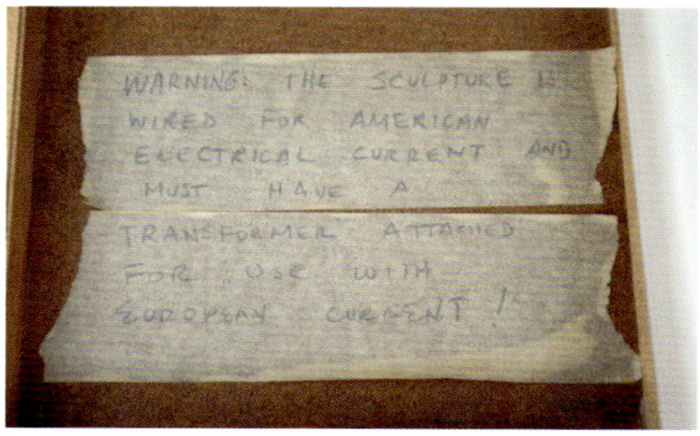
WARNING: THE SCULPTURE IS
WIRED FOR AMERICAN
ELECTRICAL CURRENT AND
MUST HAVE A
TRANSFORMER ATTACHED
FOR USE WITH
EUROPEAN CURRENT !

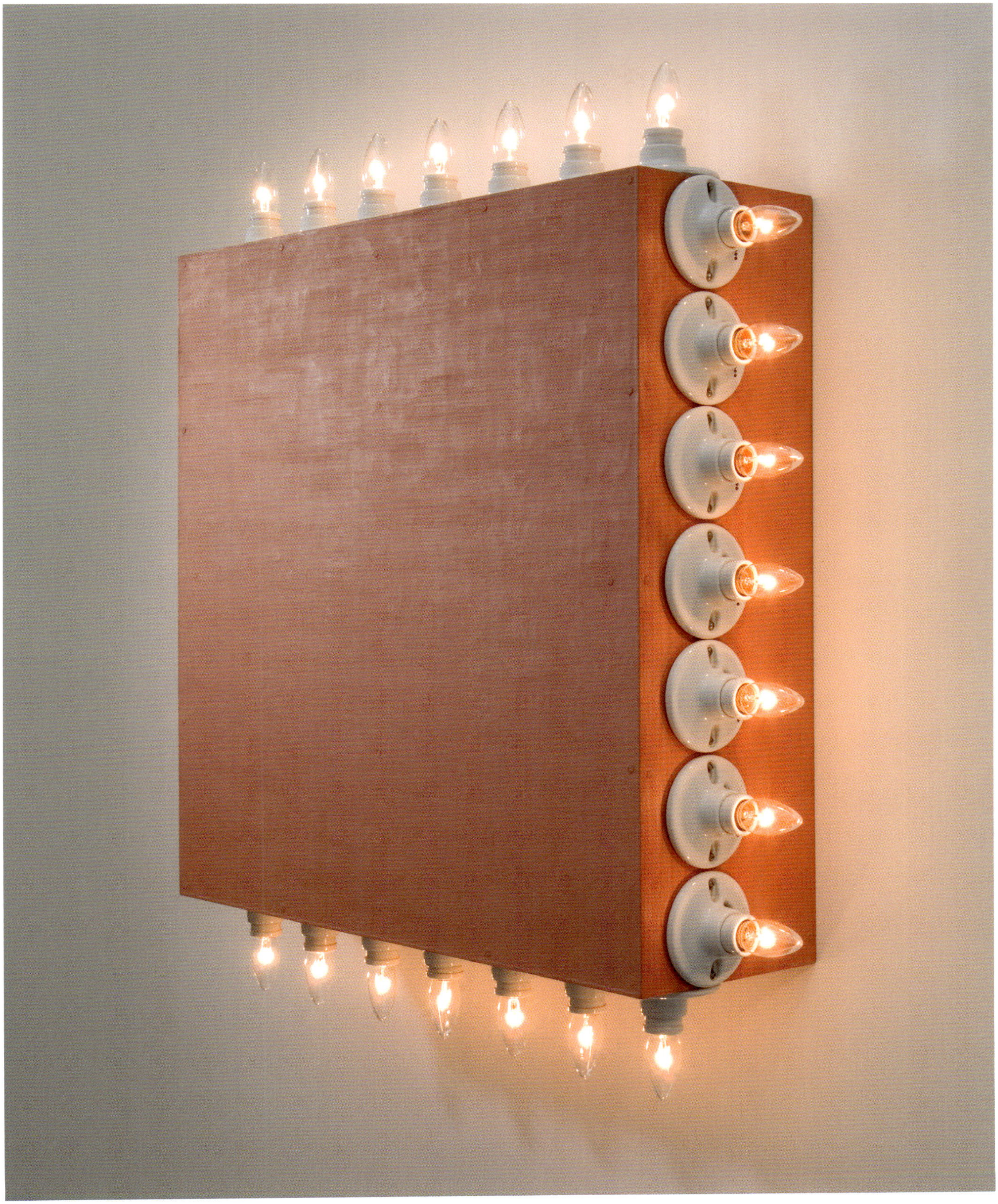

icon VI

icon VI (Ireland dying) (to Louis Sullivan) 1962–63
oil on Masonite, painted steel receptacles, glass cap,
red incandescent bulb and socket disc flasher
$25\frac{1}{4}$ x $25\frac{3}{16}$ x $10\frac{1}{4}$ in. (64.1 x 63.9 x 26 cm) excluding fixture and lamp;
approx. $25\frac{3}{4}$ x $25\frac{11}{16}$ x $10\frac{1}{4}$ in. (65.4 x 65.2 x 26 cm) including fixture and lamp

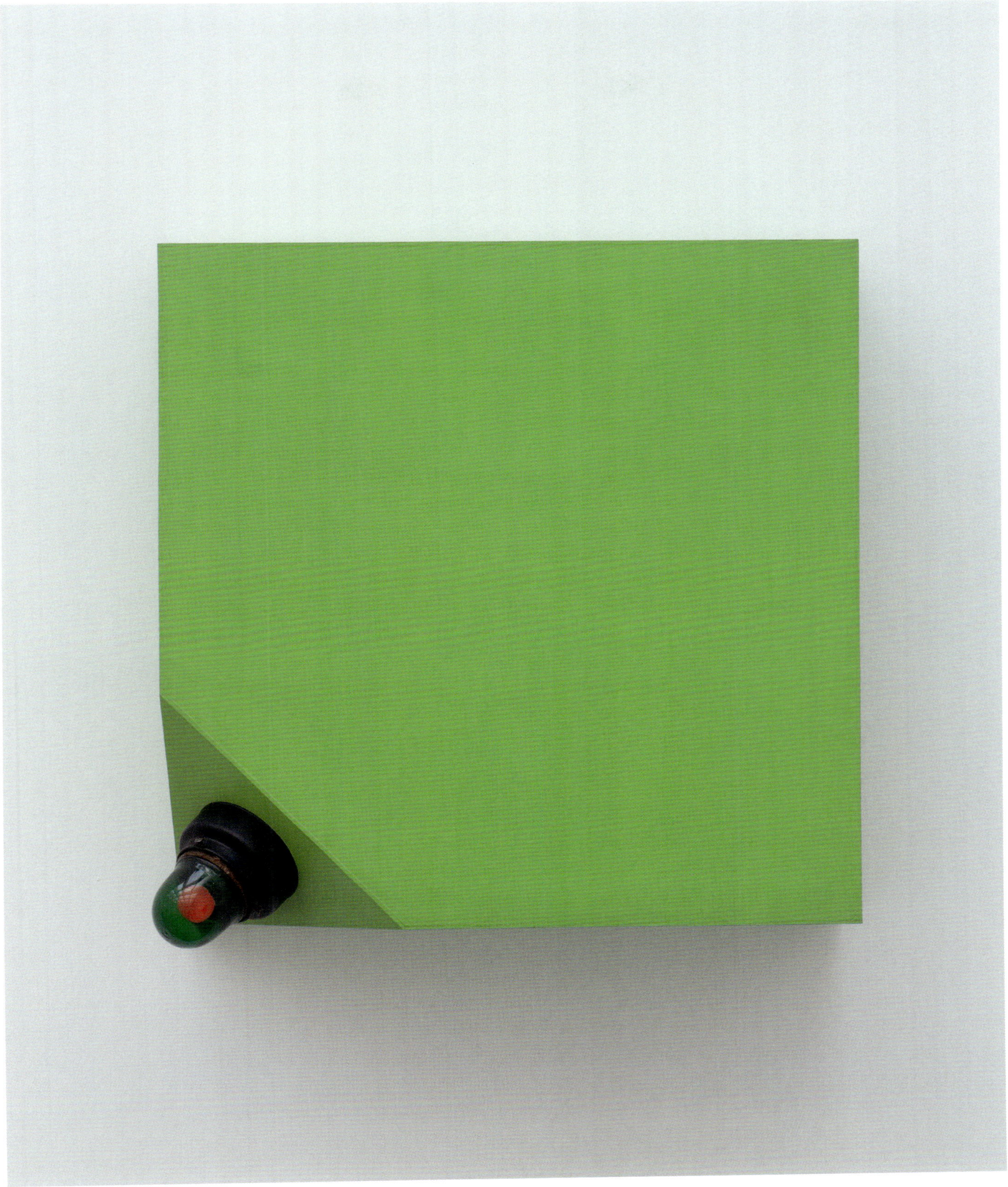

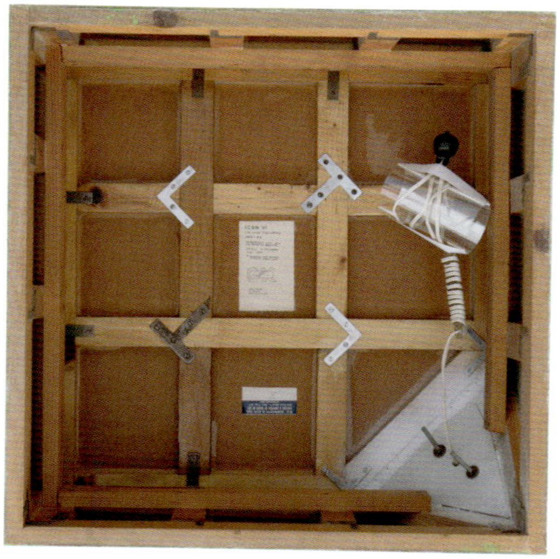

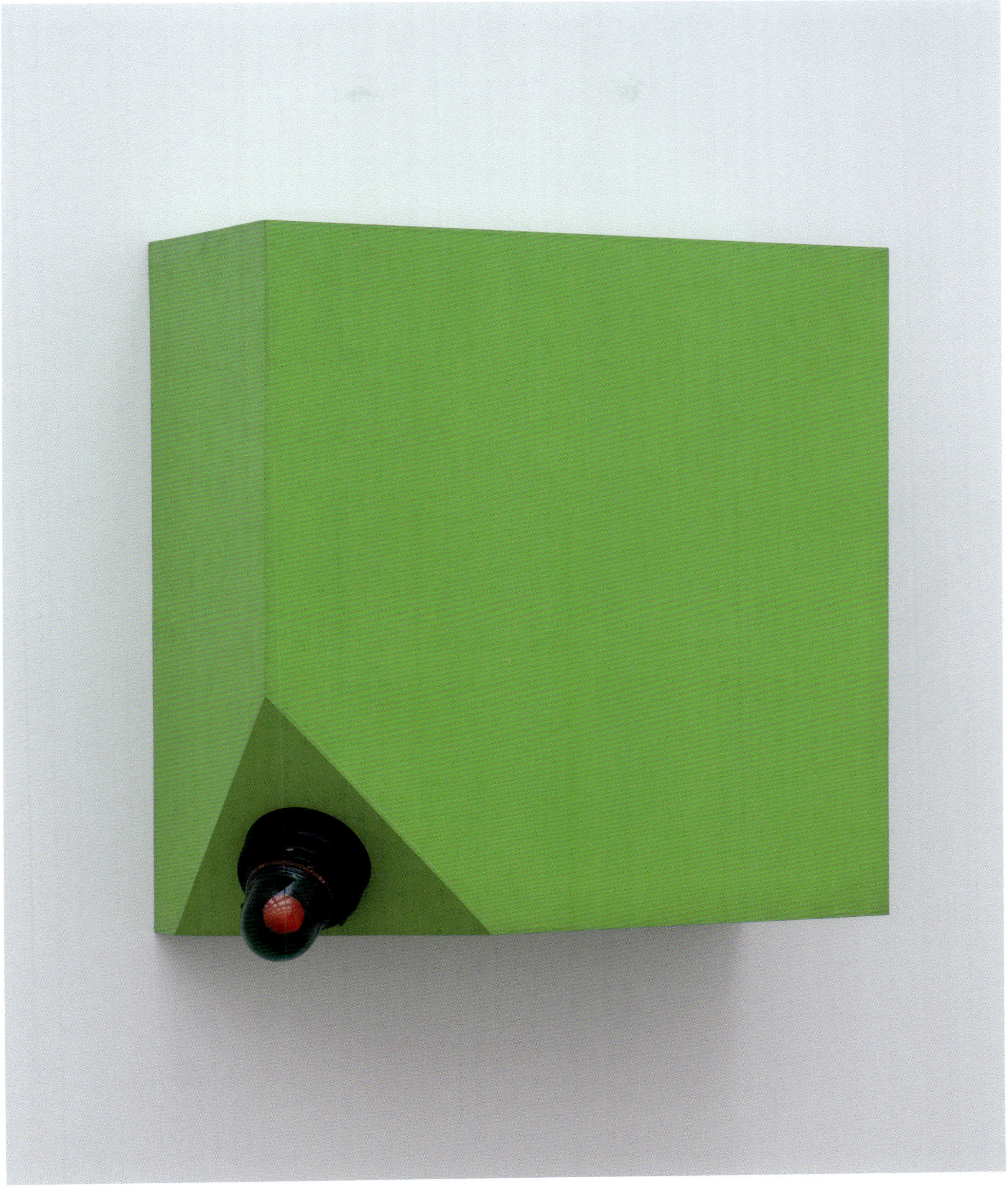

icon VII

icon VII (via crucis), 1962–64
acrylic on Masonite and daylight fluorescent light
25⅛ x 25⅛ x 10⅛ in. (63.9 x 63.9 x 25.7 cm) excluding fixture and lamp;
approx. 28 x 28 x 10⅛ in. (71.1 x 71.1 x 25.7 cm) including fixture and lamp

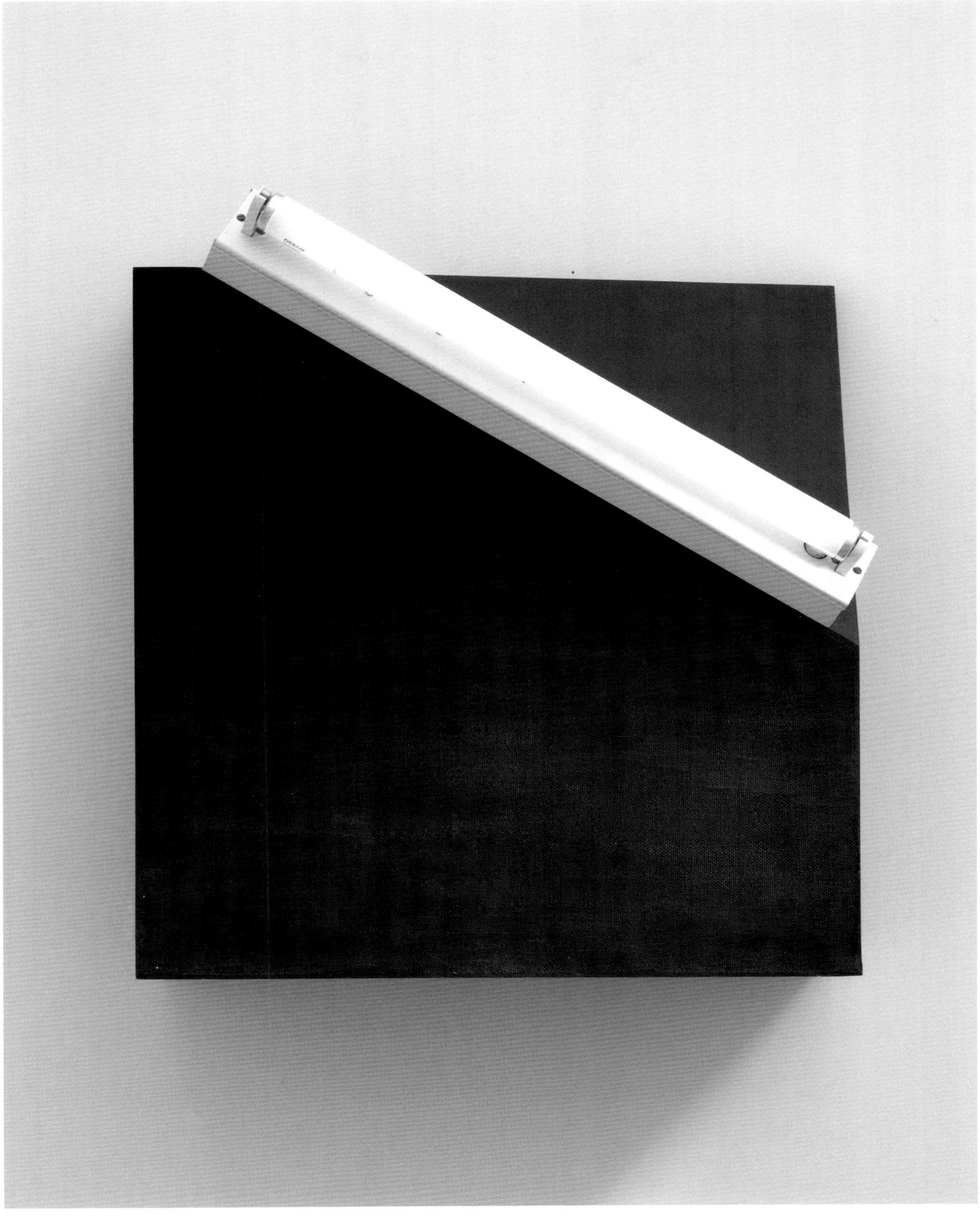

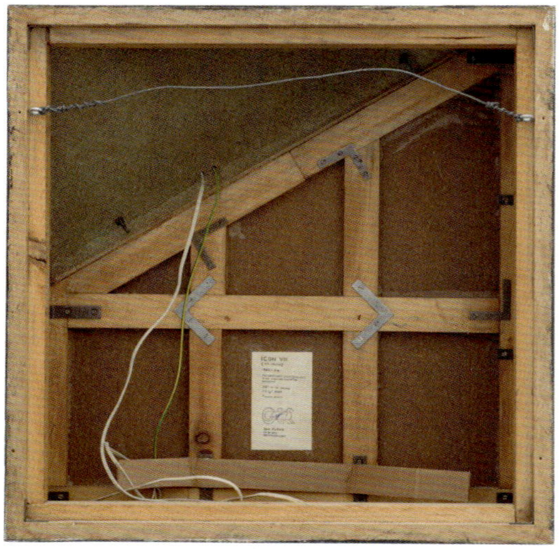

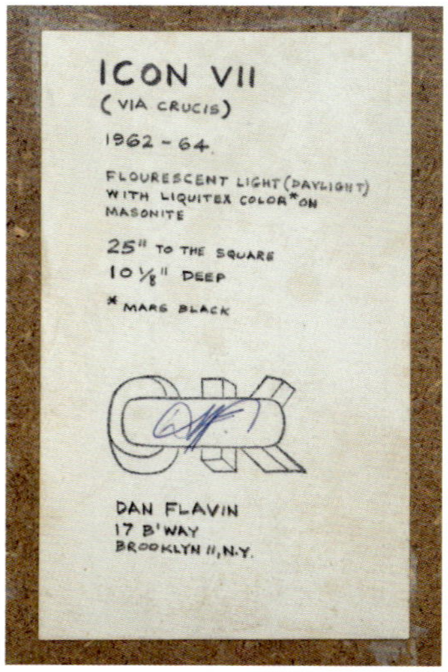
ICON VII
(VIA CRUCIS)
1962 - 64
FLOURESCENT LIGHT (DAYLIGHT)
WITH LIQUITEX COLOR* ON
MASONITE
25" TO THE SQUARE
10 1/8" DEEP
* MARS BLACK
DAN FLAVIN
17 B'WAY
BROOKLYN 11, N.Y.

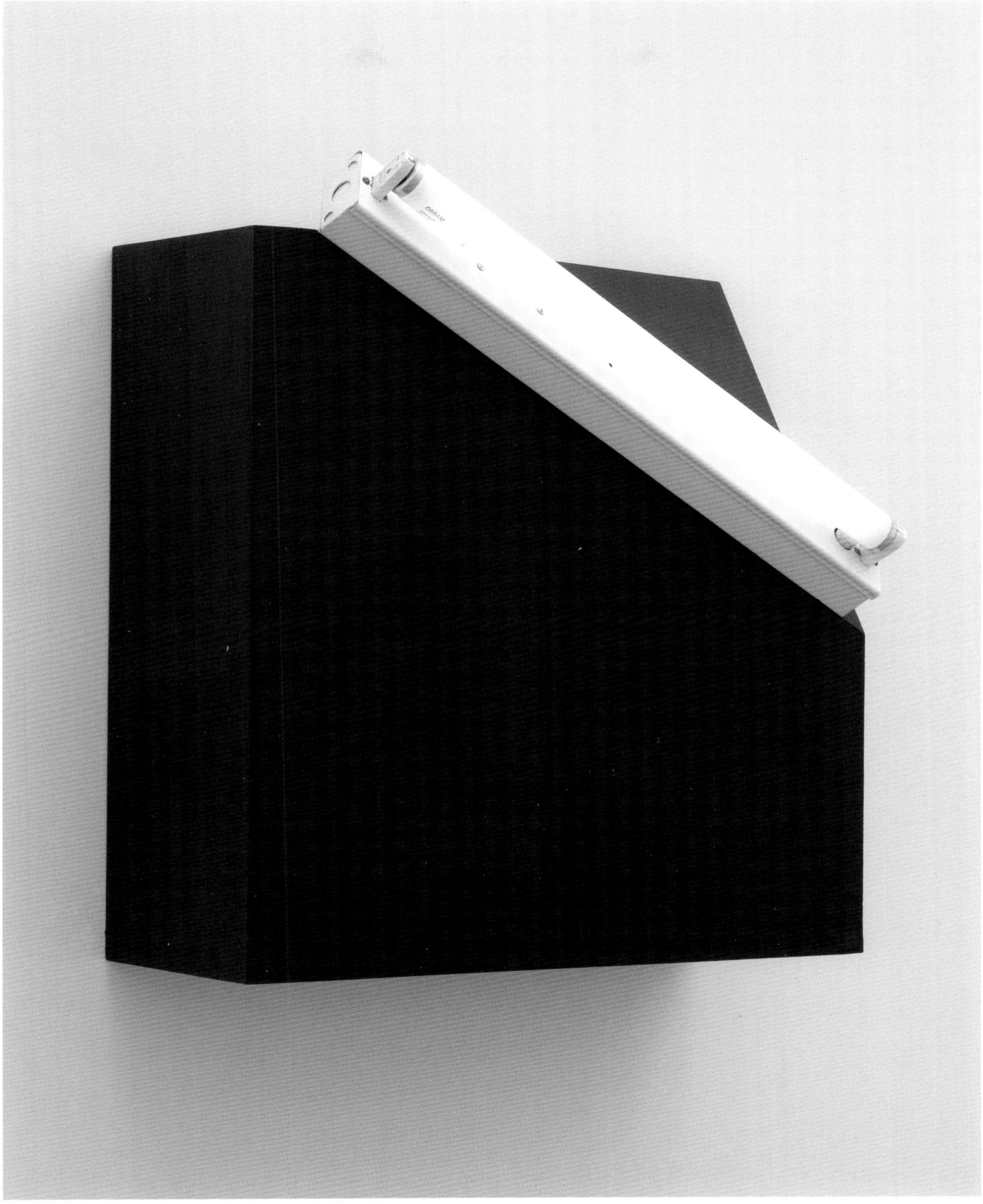

icon VIII

icon VIII (the dead nigger's icon) (to Blind Lemon Jefferson), 1962–63
oil on Masonite, porcelain receptacles, pull chains,
red incandescent bulbs, and socket disc flashers
25⅛ x 25⅛ x 10⁷⁄₁₆ in. (71.1 x 71.1 x 25.7 cm)

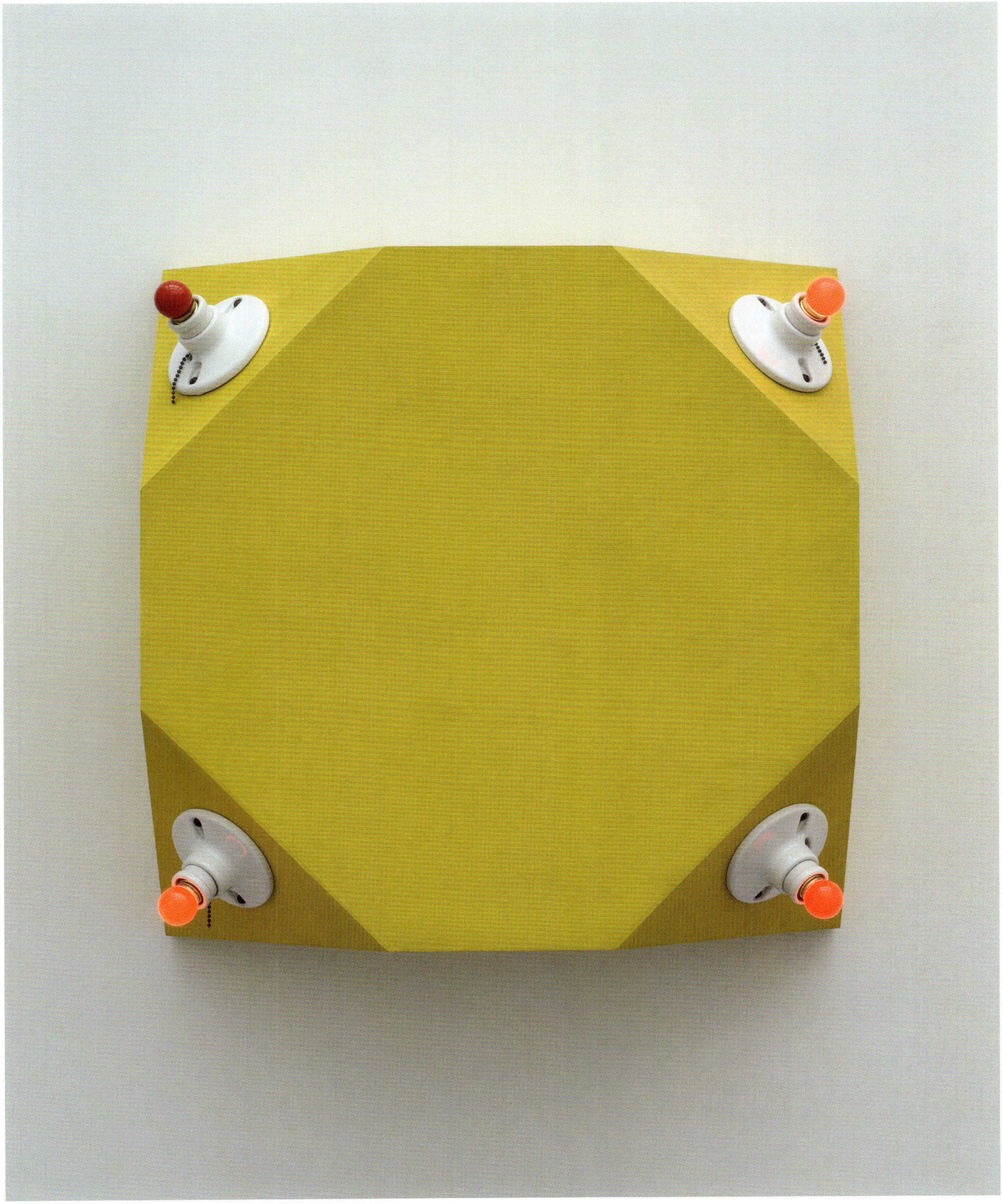

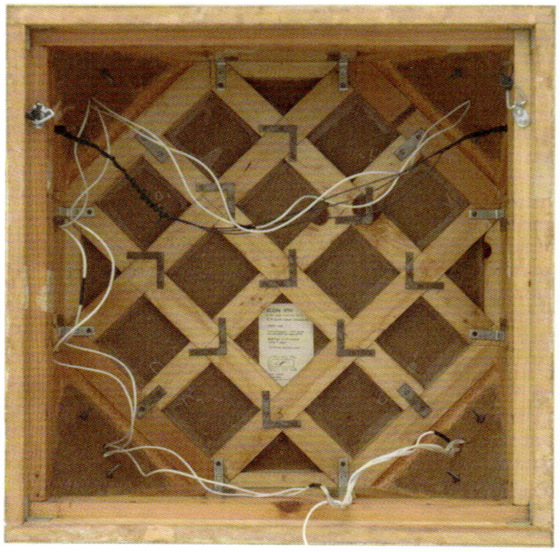

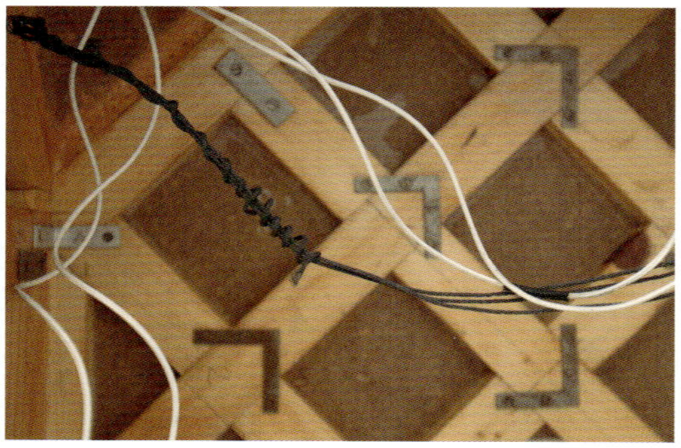

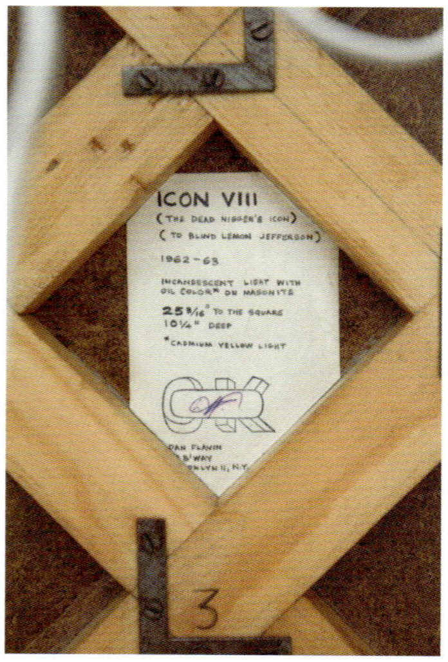
ICON VIII
(THE DEAD NIGGER'S ICON)
(TO BLIND LEMON JEFFERSON)
1962-63
INCANDESCENT LIGHT WITH OIL COLOR* ON MASONITE
25 3/16" TO THE SQUARE
10 1/4" DEEP
*CADMIUM YELLOW LIGHT
DAN FLAVIN
B'WAY
11, N.Y.
3

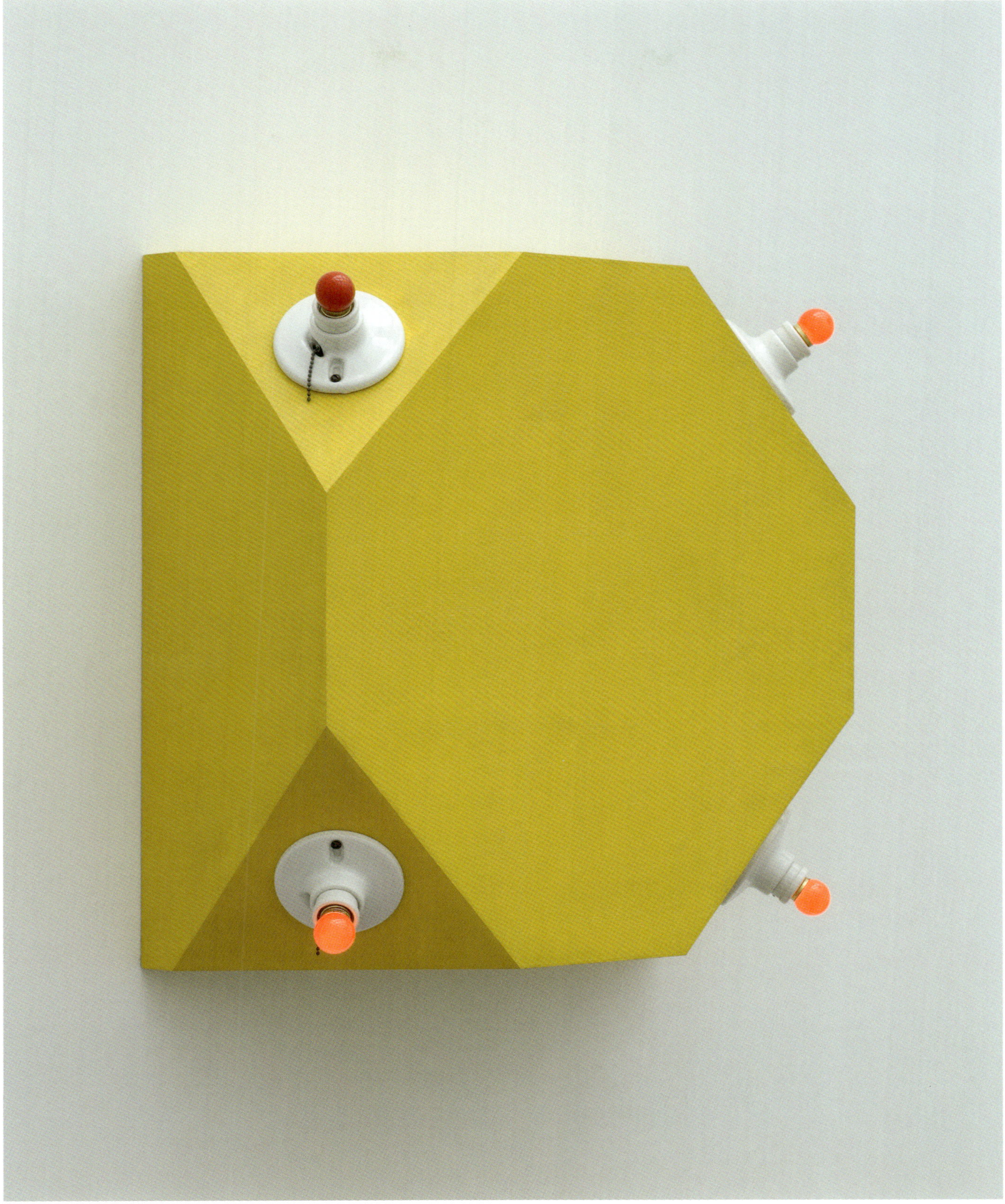

Installation Views Munich

icon V

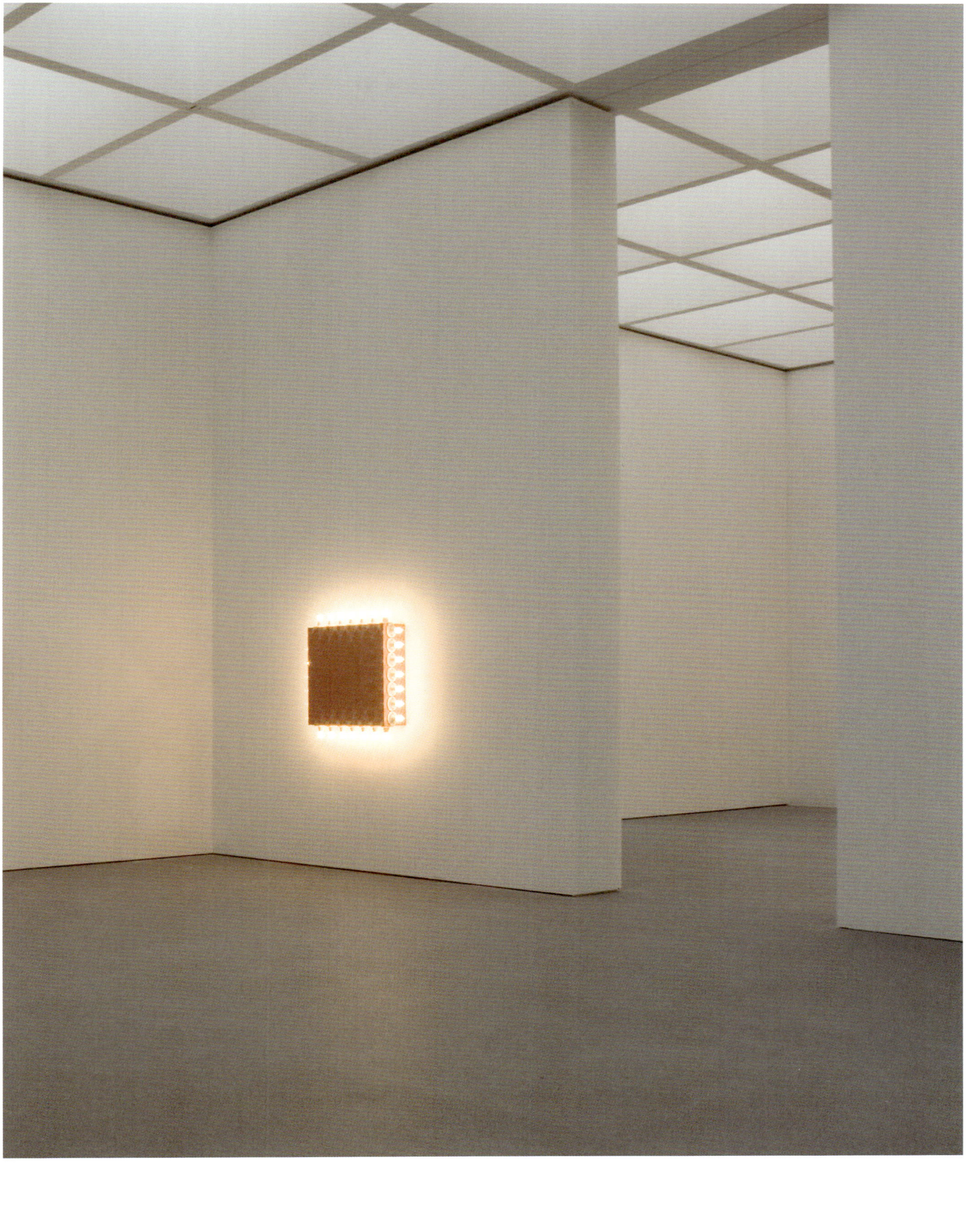

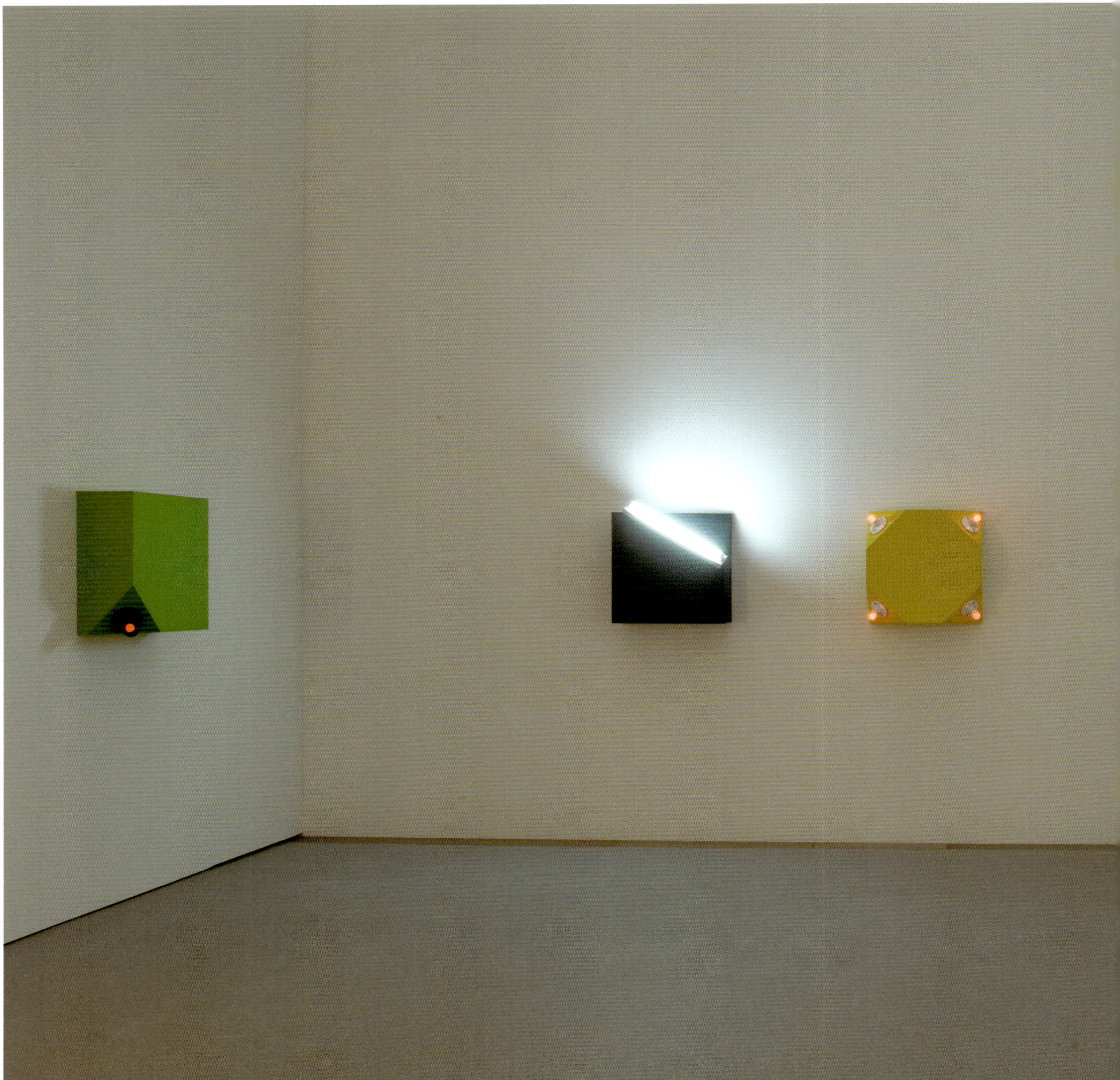

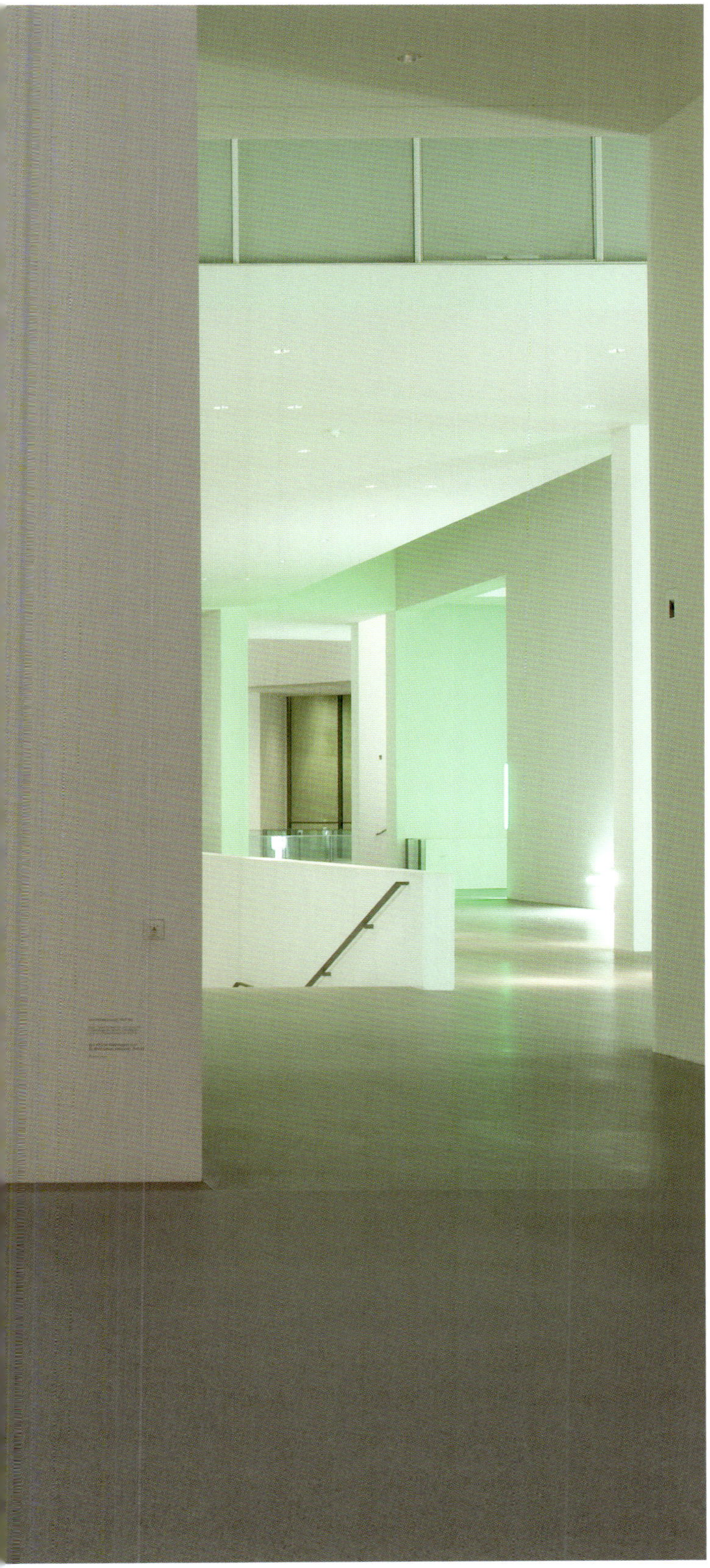

Left to right: **icon VI, icon VII & icon VIII**

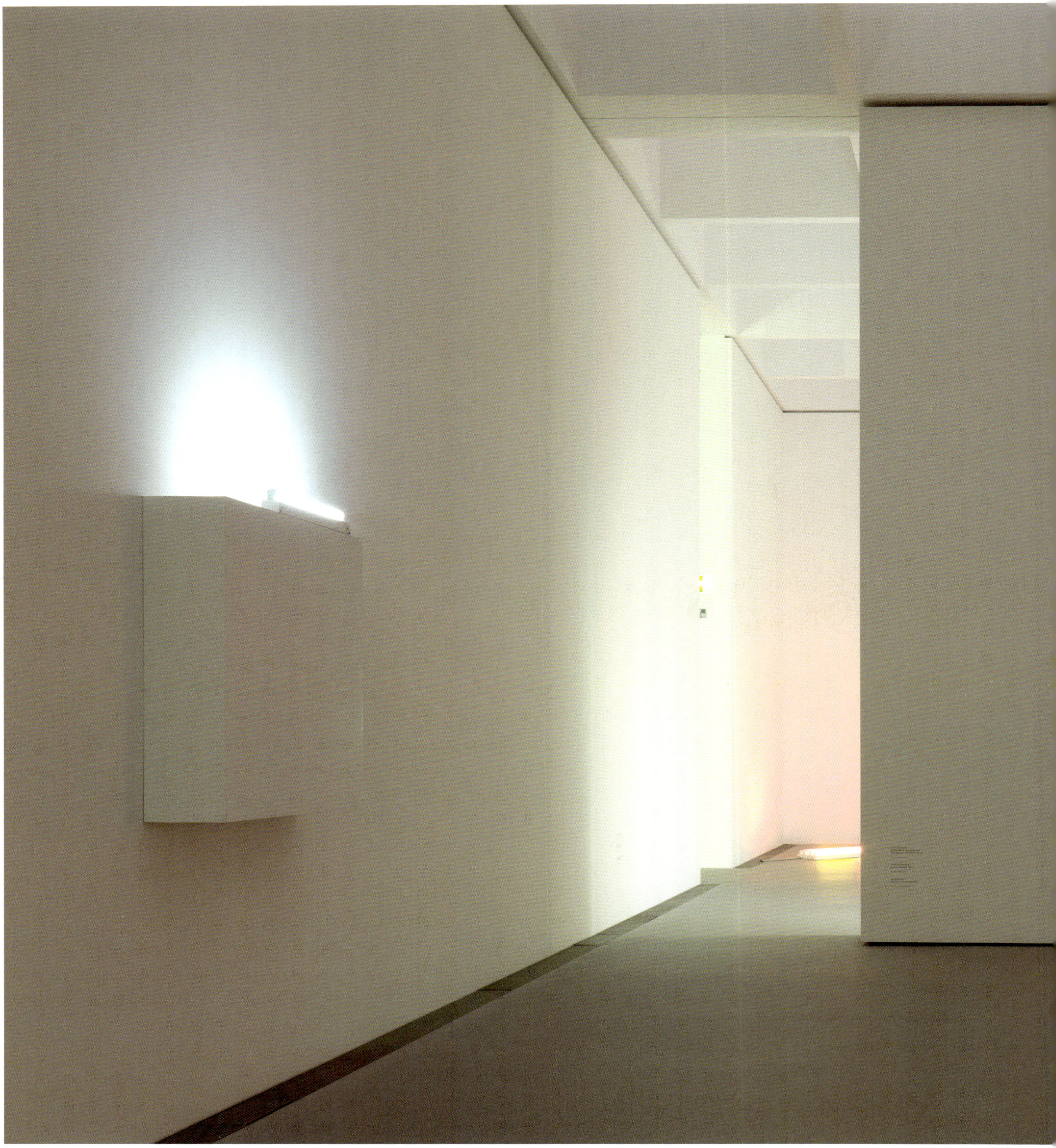

Left to right: icon IV, icon I, icon II, icon III & icon V

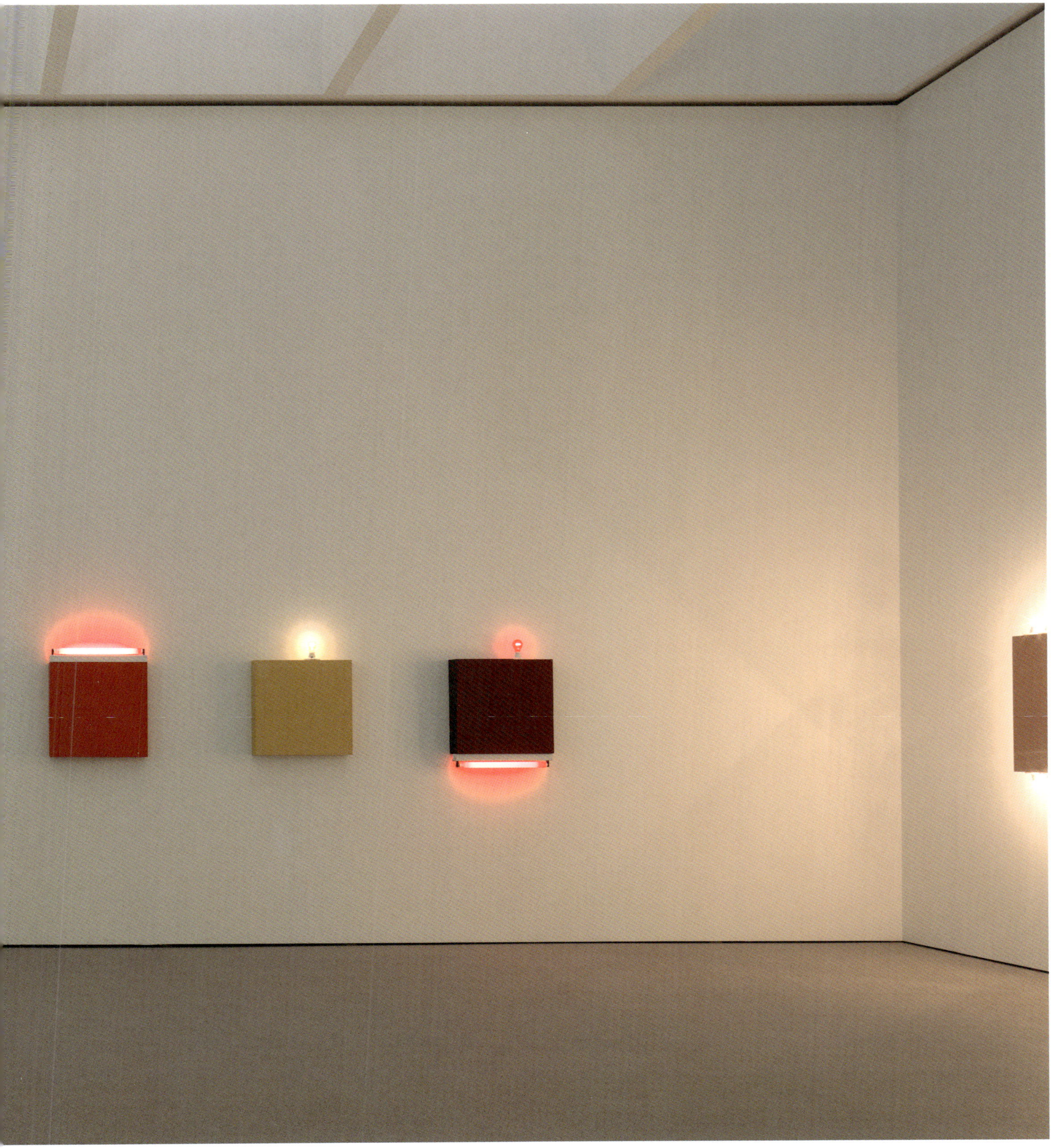

the nominal three (to William of Ockham), 1963
cool white fluorescent light
8 ft. (244 cm) high

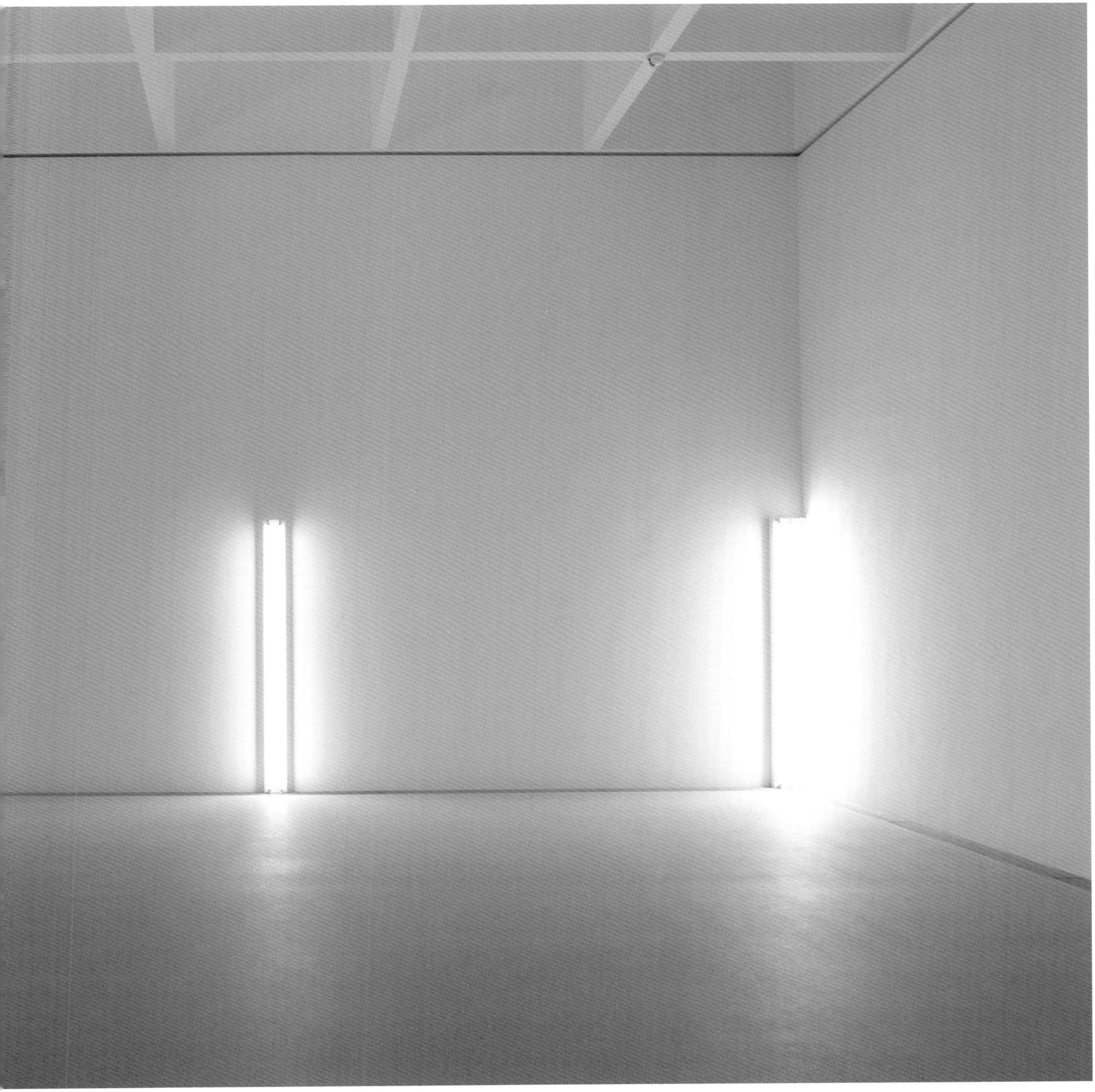

the diagonal of May 25, 1963 (to Constantin Brancusi), 1963
yellow fluorescent light
8 ft. (244 cm) long on the diagonal

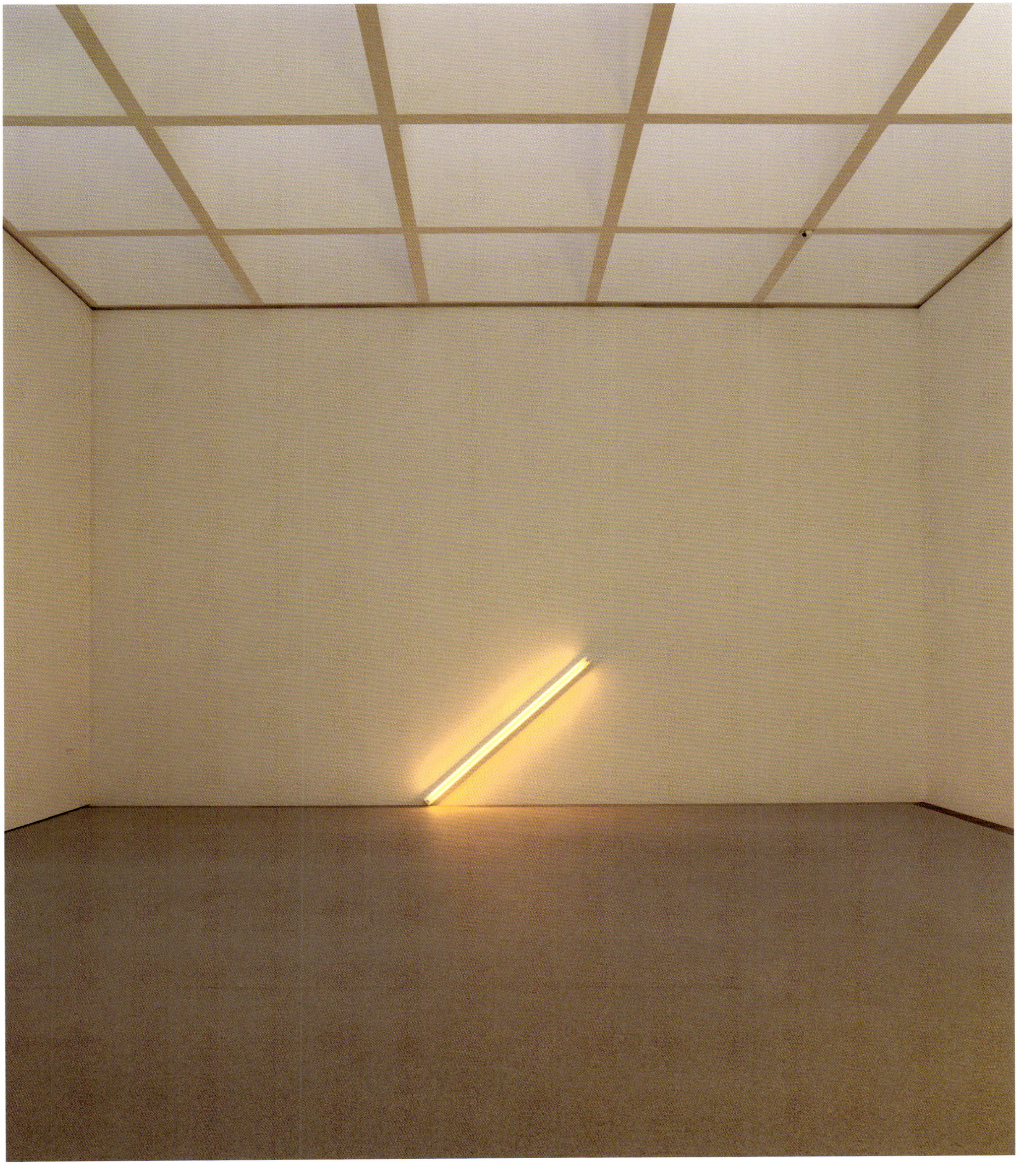

Translated from the German by Jeremy Gaines

First published in the United Kingdom in 2009
by Thames & Hudson Ltd, 181A High Holborn,
London WC1V 7QX

www.thamesandhudson.com

The photographs of the objects and the installations at the Pinakothek der Moderne, Munich, are by Haydar Koyupinar.

British Library Cataloguing-in-Publication Data
A catalogue record for this book is available
from the British Library

ISBN: 978-0-500-09351-1

Printed and bound in Germany

AMERICAN
PATRONS
OF THE
PINAKOTHEK